To Carol & Mel,

May the messages in your life be a blessing & an inspiration to you always.

Rosalie Malkiel

MESSAGES . . .

Are we listening?

Rosalie Malkiel

authorHOUSE™

1663 LIBERTY DRIVE, SUITE 200
BLOOMINGTON, INDIANA 47403
(800) 839-8640
WWW.AUTHORHOUSE.COM

First published by AuthorHouse 5/30/2006

ISBN: 1-4208-3740-0 (sc)

Library of Congress Control Number: 2005903247

Printed in the United States of America
Bloomington, Indiana

This book is printed on acid-free paper.
Cover Design by Lawrence Malkiel

Table of Contents

INTRODUCTION

Throughout my life, I have had strange experiences that have convinced me that there can be communication between God and man. I have found my life made easier by analyzing these occurrences and through them have found God to be my Therapist, Physician and Guide. This book is a journey of how I came to these conclusions. I believe that we are all capable of receiving these mystical messages if we keep the "channels open". This cannot be accomplished by attributing strange occurrences to "just coincidence". I've heard it said a coincidence is an anonymous reminder of God's existence. Just as wearing glasses enables us to see better, acknowledging God's hand in our lives serves the same purpose. It gives us insight into occurrences that we come to realize as miraculous and having a purpose. Where one person may witness an occurrence and see only the physical side of it, another, through faith, will see it through a different light. For instance, the

Egyptians lying dead on the seashore in the Book of Exodus would appear to the onlooker as though they simply drowned in the sea. The Israelites, however, witnessed the parting of the sea, which allowed them to walk on dry land. They knew that it was God that performed the miracle for them. A miracle can be described as the possible (natural phenomenon) occurring at the proper time through the Grace of God. The parting of the Red Sea and the plagues at the time of redemption of the Jewish people from Egypt are examples. There has been recent scientific data that points to the fact that these occurrences could have happened through natural phenomenon, one right after the other. The miracle was that it happened at a particular time, crucial to saving the Jewish people.

It is true that "everything" is a miracle; the pattern of a flower, the birth of a baby, the way the body works, the vastness of the Universe, etc. However, it is not miraculous if man does not acknowledge it as such. Our witness to it makes it a reality. This book will be filled with "miracles". Cynics will say they are coincidental. For these people, there can be no miracles until they open their hearts and minds to the mysterious ways in which God works. I look upon these incidents not only as miracles but messages. By analyzing our motives and actions and occurring results, we can strive to be better people. In this way, we allow the light of God to illuminate our lives. In our busy world, we are often too preoccupied to notice these messages.

Through prayer, we **send** messages, asking God's help in our every-day lives and for His guidance to always "do the right thing" as well as showing gratitude for His blessings. The Bible is a good source of **receiving** messages through its teachings of the Commandments and stories that inspire a moralistic life. Thus, with prayer and bible study, we have an on-going communication of talking and listening.

Have you ever had a strange, mystical experience or an encounter with ESP? Have you ever met that "special" person and believed that your meeting was due to fate or coincidence? When you experience disappointment, are you able to look back and see that "it all worked out for the best" or do you harbor bitterness? Upon tackling a problem that seems to have no solution, do you pray to the Lord for help and then suddenly discover an answer that is very simple and was right before your eyes all the time? There is a parallel to this mentioned in the Bible in Genesis. It relates how Hagar, Abraham's handmaid watched her son dying of thirst in the wilderness and prayed. God opened her eyes to a nearby well that was there all the time!

A strange incident occurred to me when looking for a title for this book.

One Saturday night, I attended a dance with my husband. We had been quarreling over some trivial thing and I was carried away by foolish anger. As

I sat at the table frowning, my mind wandered to my friend who had recently lost her father unexpectedly. I pondered how precarious life could be. Just a few moments later, people began running over to the DJ asking for an ambulance. A man had apparently suffered a heart attack at one of the tables. I then realized how foolish we both had been by arguing over something so trivial. I thought, "What if this terrible tragedy occurred to one of us and we had been angry at each other at the last?" My friend, Carole, a dear, long-time friend of mine, always uses the phrase, "Life is too short to be angry". I realized as I returned home that night that my presence at the dance had taught me a great lesson. It served as a reminder. "Yes," I thought to myself as I went downstairs to transfer the wash to the dryer, "The experience this evening was a "message". That's it! "Messages" describes perfectly the incidents in my book. Just after the thought struck me, I reached into the washing machine to pick up a sweater to read the drying instructions. On the label and there in bold print was the manufacturer's name "MESSAGES". I believe I actually received a message to call my book "Messages".

Chapter 1
IN THE BEGINNING

A MIRACLE BIRTH

It was the spring of 1938 when Frieda Jasper married Morris Lishinsky. They were both Russian Jewish immigrants. It was not the first marriage for either of them. Being both on in years, they did not hesitate to start a family, even though they were poverty stricken. Frieda's ill health presented another problem. After learning she was pregnant, she was strongly advised by her doctor to abort the pregnancy. He felt that the stress of pregnancy and labor would be a great burden on her rheumatic heart. With much courage and faith in God, she chose to go through with the pregnancy. The months passed with no problem. As the delivery date drew near, contractions began and she entered the hospital only to be told to return home. "False labor", the attending nurse informed her. When she returned to her Bronx flat, she was shortly delivered of a baby girl, unattended by a nurse or physician. The ambulance came soon after and the attendant tied the umbilical cord.   Mother and baby were doing fine, Baruch Hashem (Blessed be the name of God!) I was born on the 18th day of January. In Hebrew, the number 18 signifies life. My daughter, in her biology class informed me that the heart of a fetus starts beating on the 18th day of life. Had my mother not had that trust in God, I would not be here to write about this. I once heard a rabbi, in one of his sermons, define a miracle as a sign of God's love and trust. He went on to say that the miracle is not complete unless we acknowledge it. This seems to indicate that both God and man must work together to obtain the ultimate results. I owe the miracle of my existence to that love and trust between God and man. (In this case, between God and woman!)

THE BEGINNING OF FAITH

As an infant, there was not even enough money to buy a crib for me.   I slept in a drawer, as did Peewee in the Popeye cartoon! As time went by, my mother's health did not improve. By the time I was five years old, my mother suffered a heart attack. I was aware that my father was also not in the best of health. Even at this young age, I was terrified of being left alone in the world. My mother urged me to pray. This is my first recollection of my attempt to communicate with God. I attribute the setting of the foundations of my faith in God to my mother's religious beliefs and observances. I prayed that my parents would live at least long enough to see me grow up. I remember feeling a chill go through my body as I prayed. My prayer was answered, for my parents not only lived to see me grow up and get married, but also were able to enjoy several grandchildren, Baruch Hashem (Blessed be God!) When we pray, we are sending messages **to** God and when we study the Bible, we are **receiving** messages on how to live a good life.

My faith deepened as I grew older. At the young age of seventeen, I felt the great responsibility of financially supporting my aged, sick parents. During my junior high school years, my teachers were encouraging me to write. I wrote poetry and articles for the school paper. I wanted to be a writer. My Aunt Minnie, God rest her soul, made me realize that at that time, it would not be practical. Our family needed financial support and we wanted to get off the stigma and hardship of public assistance. I enrolled in a vocational high school for secretarial studies. The subject did not initially interest me, but as I studied, I realized it wasn't that bad. At graduation, I was informed that my grades would enable me to receive a college scholarship. I reluctantly refused and applied for a job as a secretary in Manhattan. I remember my knees shaking as I sat in the outer office waiting to be interviewed. I was tested and received the job, but the following week was a nightmare for me. I felt the pressure of the importance of keeping this job. It meant so much to my parents and to me. I was so nervous that I could not eat. I was quite thin and could not keep food down. I went to a local family doctor. He listened as I complained how strict and hovering my parents were with me since I was an only child. I felt this contributed to my nervousness. He wisely asked me: "Would you rather have parents that neglect you or ones that love and care so much about you?" I realized how ungrateful I had been about their concern for my welfare. The doctor suggested tranquilizers to calm me down. The thought of taking pills seemed like a crutch to me and only a temporary solution for I did not want to depend on tranquilizers every time I had stress in my life. I needed more stability. I remember leaving the office that night and staring up at the starlit sky and having a feeling of peace and oneness with God. I no longer resented my parent's strict upbringing, but was grateful that God had given me such caring parents. I prayed and began to read the Bible. I found books that would help me to have a better understanding of my religion. My mother kept Sabbath and we kept kosher but I was not familiar with other Jewish laws and customs. I found (and continue to find) much wisdom in the Torah, which is basically the Old Testament (The Five Books of Moses). Through it, I learned more about the commandments (613) and it became my mainstay. I also found reading the prophets and proverbs a great guide for every-day living. To "love mercy, do justice and follow His Commandments" sums it up for me! By pursuing this path, I found an inner peace. I prayed that God would give me the strength and wisdom to keep the job that I had. Meanwhile, my boss was beginning to be concerned about my ability to fulfill the position. Unknown to me at the time, his other secretary, Virginia, insisted that he give me more time. She felt that I had potential. My prayers were answered through her kindness toward me. God bless her soul, as she is no longer with us! In due time, I was able to perform my secretarial duties quite well.

As time went on, I applied my newfound strength to my every-day problems. Whenever I was in a tense situation, and became extremely nervous, I would pray to calm myself down. I was secure in the decision of not using tranquilizers as a crutch and God became my therapist!

MEETING MAX

After working at the engineering company for five years, I became restless, wondering if I would ever meet "Mr. Right". My 18-year old friend had just become engaged and I remember her saying, "If a girl is not married by the age of 25, the chances of her ever marrying after that are very small." That was the summer of 1960, when people, in general, got married at a much younger age than they do now. I was then twenty-one years old. Seeing people at work getting married all around me and remembering my friend's remark, I felt like I was heading down "Old Maid's Lane", even at that young age.

I had been "going steady" with a few men but it did not work out. Being out in the working world and having the responsibility of supporting myself, my Mom and Dad and helping them when they were ill helped me to grow up quickly. I was "ready" to get married and my job was beginning to bore me. However, it was always in the back of my mind that whomever I married would have to agree to help me support my parents financially. This would be a burden for any young man and I was prepared to have to work while I was married until it would be no longer practical.

I was about to go on vacation in August of that year, when my father told me he had met an elderly couple in the park nearby. They had an unmarried son that was an engineer and wanted to know if he could call me. "Another blind date that doesn't work out? No!" I answered vehemently. Besides, I thought I might meet someone on my vacation in Florida. I was planning to go with a girlfriend from work. The two weeks in Florida proved fruitless. I was quite depressed on my return, although I enjoyed Florida. I prayed to God that He help to find someone right for me, and if that was not in His cards for me, that He give me the strength to be able to live alone if that became necessary. Unknown to me, at about the same time, someone else was praying a similar prayer. Only his prayer experience was more dramatic for he said he saw a "white light"! After praying, I resignedly gave my Dad the OK to tell the engineer to call me. I did not really think much would come of it. In Judaism, there are three obligations that parents have toward their children; 1) teach them to swim 2) see that they learn a skill to be able to be independent 3) do their best to see that their children marry. I will never forget that my father was instrumental in helping to find my soul mate!

When Max did call, I surmised from his phone conversation, that the only thing I thought we had in common was that I worked for an engineering company and that he was an engineer. However, he sounded very pleasant on the phone. We set a date for the following Sunday afternoon.

It was a hot summer day at the end of August. I wore a green sheath chiffon dress. When I answered the doorbell of our Bronx apartment, I was stunned! The image I had of the person that I would marry was standing in front of me! I always dreamt that he would have blue eyes, light curly hair, good body build, fine features and wear glasses! After greeting him, I dashed to the back room to say good-bye to my mother as she gathered the positive vibes from me. "Wow!" I commented to her as I left for my date.

Max also lived in the Bronx just a few blocks from my apartment. On our first date, we decided to go to the Bronx Botanical Gardens. We both liked the outdoors and nature. It was a hot, sunny day and we sat down on a bench to eat ice cream. I insisted that he not sit in the hot sun and moved over on the bench so that he would be in the shade. Of course, being a gentleman, he refused to do so. At a later time, he informed me that this seemingly insignificant gesture showed that I was a caring person. Unknowingly, I guess I passed my test! There is a similar "test" in the Bible when Abraham's servant is sent to secure a wife for Issac. Rebecca offers him water at the well and also waters his camels. This "test" proved she was a caring person suitable to be a wife for Isaac.

We seemed quite compatible but I was still nervous. "What if he doesn't like me?" I thought. By the time evening came, and we were going to a deli to eat dinner, I was a wreck. I was prone to getting a nervous stomach when under stress. The smell of the food made me nauseous and I choked. "Waiter!" Max shouted. "There should be water on the table!" In contrast to another boyfriend I had been with in a similar situation, Max was caring for me. (I guess he passed his test also!) The previous boyfriend just made me feel quite uncomfortable and I became more nervous. Max's concern for my welfare calmed me down. We then went to a nearby movie. He said he would call me again in two weeks because he had previously made reservations upstate for the following weekend. "Yea, right!" I thought! He's dumping me! He gave me a gentlemanly kiss goodnight... on the forehead!

I did not expect to hear from him again. Surprisingly he did call two weeks later. (After he staked out the Catskills for the last time, he decided that I was a good choice after all!) After that, we dated frequently, about twice a week. Just before Rosh Hashana (The Jewish New Year), which was only a few weeks later, we decided that we were going to be married. Max suggested that we get engaged on the New Year, but I preferred to wait till after the 10 days of Judgment (from Rosh Hashana to Yom Kippur), the Day of Atonement, which is a very solemn fast day. After fasting, when Yom Kippur was over, I received a beautiful ring that evening. After 45 years of marriage, I sometimes stare at it in disbelief that it belongs to me: a symbol of a promise of love everlasting. I found out years later from reading the Chumash

(The Old Testament) that the eve after Yom Kippur was traditional in biblical history for the men to go out in the field to claim the women that they would choose as their wife. It is strange that we chose this night. B'shercht!, I say (Meant to be). Both Max and I prayed for a soul mate and the good Lord heard us!

Chapter 2

THE CHILDREN

SUSAN

A TIME TO LAUGH; A TIME TO CRY

Since I was an only child and Max felt that he was getting "older", (Thirty-one in those days was already considered bachelor age) we were eager to start a family. Soon after we were married, I became pregnant. We were so happy!

In my third month of pregnancy, we decided to take a trip to Colorado. When I first started dating Max, he conveyed to me that the girl that he would marry would have to agree to move to Denver, if necessary. From way back, he had this dream about living there, although he had never been there before. Even though this meant that I would have to leave my aged, sick parents, I agreed, remembering the Bible quotation from Ruth "Wither thou goest, I shall go!" Max's vacation was due and I thought this would be a good time for him to find out once and for all if he really wanted to live there.

We traveled by train across the country. Max was not eager to fly unless it was necessary and he thought we would get a better view of the country by train. It was a very long, grueling ride and the train went mostly through many fields and the back of towns. By the time we arrived in Denver, morning sickness (it was more like morning, noon and night sickness!) took over. We went to the top of Pikes Peak in the middle of June to find snow on the ground while down below it was 80 degrees. We spent one night in a lodge on the side of a steep mountain. I remember waking to the heady smell of pines. Max scheduled a trip in a jeep that would climb through a very steep mountain. That day I stayed in my room. I was feeling more and more nauseous as the trip progressed. I could not stand the sight or smell of any food and the only thing I craved was apple pie (Not the most nutritious food). Finally, when we boarded the train to return home, Max's comment on living in Colorado was: "It's beautiful, but too mountainous for me." I think he also was not anxious to leave his old, sick parents either. When I returned home, I continued my job as a full-time secretary commuting from our Queens apartment to Manhattan. Even though Max helped me a lot, I found cooking, shopping, and cleaning difficult since I was not feeling well.

Shortly afterward, I suffered a miscarriage. This came as a shock to me as it must to every mother-to-be that has lost a baby. It left me wondering if I would ever be able to have children. My obstetrician assured me that it was not an unusual occurrence and that it was nature's way of getting rid of an imperfect fetus. I remember my neighbor's remark: "The time is not right."

I left the hospital on July 2, 1961, being escorted to the door in a wheelchair by a nurse. I watched mothers being wheeled out holding their babies while my arms were empty as I fought to hold back tears.

In October of that year, I became pregnant again and hindsight cautioned me to take it easy. No more long trips were scheduled and I decided to quit my job although we could have used the extra income. Max agreed to subsidize my parents financially. My boss would have liked me to stay, but I felt that the life of my baby came first.

I prayed that everything would be all right. The pregnancy and delivery went smoothly and Susan was born June 27, 1962. On July 2, 1962, which was <u>exactly</u> one year to the date that I had been discharged after having a miscarriage, I was wheeled out of the same hospital, this time with my arms full, holding beautiful baby Susan! Blessed be God!

As Susan was growing up, she proved to be quite intelligent and creative. She was very good in art, designing and sewing. She graduated high school at the top of her class in the business program. Soon after, she became a legal secretary in a top-notch law firm.

A PRAYING MANTIS

At the age of 18, Sue chose to move out of the house. With her high-salaried job she was financially independent. She had become involved in an abusive relationship. When I spoke to her boss, he informed me that at times, Sue would come to work with black and blue marks on her. Because of his jealous nature, except for going to work, she became a virtual prisoner of her boyfriend. We felt helpless. Since she was no longer a minor, according to the law, Sue herself would have to take action against him. This situation continued for five horrendous years. Many nights I would lie awake in bed, staring at a picture that Sue had painted. In the dim light shining from the hallway, I could see the large brown eyes of the doe in the painting. The tears rolled down my face for the painting reminded me of Sue's beautiful brown eyes. I often wondered if she was alive or dead. My prayers for her safety would finally lull me to sleep.

It was a week before the High Holidays and Max and I were making the cemetery pilgrimage to our parent's graves as was customary at this time. In the past, on these occasions, I would engage one of the Rabbis that were waiting around at the gates of the cemetery to perform the memorial prayers for the deceased. Max reminded me that it has more meaning if you do the prayers yourself, personally. Prayer book in hand, I walked to my parent's gravesite with this intention. I placed myself between the two graves. As I was praying, my husband brought to my attention that directly in front of me, perched on the shrubbery, was a praying mantis! "Do you know why it's called a praying mantis?" he asked. He answered his own question with "because the front legs are bent together like it is praying". I looked down at this little creature. He did not move from his place the whole time I was praying. I moved over to the headstone to place the traditional pebble on top to mark my presence at the grave. I continued praying; this time, spontaneously. Mr. Praying

Mantis did not move the whole time during my prayers and only moved when I was through. I have heard it said that when we pray at the graves of our ancestors that the souls of our dead relatives plea to God on our behalf. Was the praying mantis an "angel" sent to help my prayers transcend to heaven?

PRAYERS FULFILLED

Just a short time after I had been to the cemetery, I began to see things happen that gave me hope that my prayers might be answered after all these years. One day, my son, Larry, noticed a newspaper ad of a psychologist who specialized in helping people in bad relationships. If I had presented it to Susan, of course, she would not listen, but coming from a sibling, it was more palatable. She started seeing the therapist during her lunch hour and before you know it, she had decided that she MUST find a way to end her relationship! I have a dear friend who offered to hide her in her house until things simmered down. Susan's boss drove her from Manhattan to my friend's house. She stayed there for two weeks. My friend and her family took the risk of keeping her, for if he knew where she was it could have been a dangerous situation for them. She eventually rented an apartment in a different area. I thank God this marked the end of the relationship. My prayers were answered through my son, the psychologist, my friends, and Sue's boss, who all helped do God's work on earth by caring.

I hope that the telling of this episode will help some young person out there to avoid pitfalls. Even though Max and I tried many times to persuade Sue to avoid this relationship, she ignored our advice. In Judaism, besides honoring ones parents, a mother and father are believed to be God's representatives on earth, to care for and guide their children. So value their wisdom. You will avoid a lot of bad, horrible experiences that could sometimes be fatal. You may think you know it all; ' parents are old-fashioned, what do they know', but remember they have been living on this earth much longer than you. Along the way they have picked up a lot of wisdom along with the good advice they received from *their* parents! Basic human nature does not change much from generation to generation, although lately things seem to be getting worse out there. You will be able to avoid a lot of problems if you listen to your parents! Following the God-given commandment of honoring mother and father surely will bring blessings to you and your whole family.

It took Sue a number of years to settle down, but she eventually made us very proud of her achievements. She put herself through college and graduate school. She received a doctorate in biology from Albert Einstein. During her internship, she met a very nice young man who also received his doctorate in biology.

After a courtship of two years, they became engaged.

Shortly after Sue's engagement to Howie, Max retired and was given a retirement gift of a trip to a Catskill's resort for the two of us. During my stay there, I reminisced about the last time I had been at this particular hotel. Ten years had passed since we had taken a weekend off to just get away from stress. I remembered the reassuring words of a guest there at the time. When we were discussing our families, she insisted that Sue was going to be all right and that she would get married. This woman seemed very sure about this. I gathered that she was a psychic individual, but at the time, I found it difficult to believe her. As I was thinking about this episode of the past, I stared out of our picture window at the hotel. Just at that moment, a bird came to the window, perched on the ledge a few moments and then flew away. I take the appearance of the bird as a sign of a prophecy fulfilled.

Sue and Howie were married on April 13, 1997, Baruch Hashem! It was a beautiful wedding.

Both bride and groom smiled just about through the whole ceremony.

About one year later, Mathew Gabriel was born to them. A few years after that, they gave me my first granddaughter, Ava Gayle. Both are beautiful, precocious grandchildren.

I thank God for turning the previous troublesome years into miraculous dreams come true. It taught me not to give up; to have hope, that God will help us if we come to Him.

LARRY

A CLOSE CALL

Susan was such an easy, delightful baby to care for that Max and I agreed not to wait very long for another. God had other plans, however, and my third pregnancy ended in a second miscarriage. When I became pregnant again, everything seemed to be going fine. I passed that critical third month when miscarriages usually occur.

In my fifth month, however, I started to develop severe varicose veins in my right leg. By the sixth month I was hospitalized. It was discovered that the placenta was in front of the baby and that was causing all the pressure. I remained in the hospital for the following two months restricted to my bed, so that there would be less risk of losing the baby. I was finally released in my eighth month to bed rest at home till delivery. Of course, I prayed intensely for everything to go well. I started labor three weeks early, just as I had with Susan. I went into the hospital on a Saturday night. Labor continued all through Sunday, which happened to be Father's Day. (Sorry about that, Max). Monday morning it was decided to do a Caesarian as the placenta was still blocking the baby. Larry was born that morning, June 15, 1964. He was a perfect baby, Baruch Hashem!

Larry's sister Susan welcomed him into the world with hugs and kisses and through the years they have maintained a closeness.

During Larry's childhood years, he showed great ability in all areas. The public school in our area was having major disciplinary problems and since I always wanted our children to have a religious education, we enrolled them in a Yeshiva. (Jewish religious school that teaches Hebrew, religion and the usual academic subjects that are taught in the public school system.) His grades at the Yeshiva, which had a high scholastic standing, were very good. He was also good in art and he loved music and writing. At the age of nine, he received a City-Wide Reader's Digest Poetry Award, (2nd place for his age group) on Nature. This poem, and the picture he drew that went along with it, had a great influence on my decision to have child No. 5 as you will find out later in this book. When we moved to Syosset, a suburb of Long Island, he did not have to work as hard in the public schools as he did at the Yeshiva, although Syosset has a very good reputation scholastically. He graduated Syosset High with an 89 average without ever doing much studying.

GROWING PAINS

From the age of 13 years on, Larry did not grow. He was very short and thin. He was 4'10" tall and weighed 75 lbs. A physician who specialized in nutrition treated him with vitamins and supplements. When this program showed no change, he was finally hospitalized at the age of 17. It was found that he simply was not getting enough calories to spur bone growth. He was supervised in the hospital to see that this was accomplished. By the time he left the hospital six weeks later, bone growth had begun again. Today, thank God our prayers were answered. He now stands 5' 8" and reached an average weight. While in high school, he missed out on sports and a social life. He felt it was because of his height. When he entered Stony Brook University, he tried to make up for it. While taking a tough engineering program, he partied too much and flunked himself out of school. It was a tough road trying to get back. He worked as a custodian, dishwasher, and cab driver, which was his last job when he lived in our house. He was trying to save money to return to classes in perhaps the art field. I prayed that God would give him the guidance and strength to fulfill the capabilities that He has bestowed upon him.

A LONG-LOST LOVE

When my father became too sick to handle, I had an aid come to help me. She was a pretty, black Haitian woman. Her name was Joyce. Although she was thin, she was wiry and quite strong and was a great help to me. I found her to be very easy to get along with. She was really concerned about my father and did her best to care for him. I had been under much stress in the past months caring for my father, practically single-handed. Max and I felt it would do us both good to get away for a weekend now that Joyce was here. Larry was left to take care of the rest of the family.

We went to an upstate resort in New York. When we returned home, we found that Larry had done more than take care of the family. While we were gone, he and Joyce had developed a relationship. We could see how they looked at each other that they were in love. Eventually, Joyce came to speak to me, wondering how I felt about it. I mentioned the fact that it might be difficult socially for them to fit in as a couple in society. I also felt their children might have problems in identifying to which race they belonged to. Joyce assured me that this was not as severe a problem as it was years ago, that people's attitudes have changed to some degree. She had cousins in her family that were children of inter-racial parents and she said they were well adjusted. However, the major problem that upset me, personally, was the fact that Joyce was not Jewish. In our faith, a marriage cannot take place in Jewish law, if both parties are not Jewish. Joyce would have to convert, which she agreed to, surprisingly, for I thought she was a devout Christian.

However, Larry was not progressing financially enough to get married at the time. Eventually Joyce married a construction worker and moved out to California with him. The standard of living in California at that time seemed better for housing and salary for the couple. Also, Joyce preferred the warm climate.

Years went by and Larry never forgot Joyce. To the best of my knowledge, he did not date anyone else seriously. They occasionally exchanged greeting cards across the miles. About 5 years went by. Joyce's husband, Will, started a   business and it began to flourish. Unfortunately, his health began to deteriorate. When it was revealed that he had AIDS, Joyce knew that it would not be an easy road in helping him, since she had taken care of several AIDS patients in the past. Joyce dauntlessly cared for him throughout his illness but after five years, he finally succumbed. Even though it was difficult to witness Will's suffering when he was alive, it was just as hard for Joyce to deal with her grief over losing him. She turned to Larry for consolation. After a while, Larry took a trip out to California and the relationship was rekindled. The Passover holidays were approaching and Larry wanted Joyce to get a "taste" of Judaism by inviting her to the family Seder. She enjoyed it very much and on the second Seder evening, she joined us for the invitation at our Rabbi's house, also. She seemed quite interested in knowing about the rituals and the reasons for them. It was still my hope that she would convert to Judaism, but I did not know how she felt about it. To my surprise she was still willing to convert which meant taking a lengthy conversion course as a requirement. It was also necessary for Larry to attend these classes with her which he did. Joyce enjoyed the classes and found Judaism to be a very sensible religion. She completed the course and Larry and "Tsippy" became engaged. Tsippy (short for Zipporah) was Joyce's choice of her new name in Hebrew. Zipporah in the Bible was the wife of Moses. It is customary for a convert to Judaism to take on a new name in Hebrew, symbolic of beginning a new life. Tsippy insisted that she be called by her new name. She followed the rituals with enthusiasm, more so than my son who had to be coaxed by her to attend synagogue on Shabbat. If this is not a story about fate, I don't know what is! Ten years of waiting!

They were married on Long Island a year later. It was a beautiful wedding. The families on both sides of the family got along very well with each other. I have known weddings, in the past, where the families of the bride and groom, that were of the same race, did not want to speak to each other. During the reception, the air-conditioning broke down in the middle of a hot July day! The Haitian-born relatives, of course, did not seem to mind the heat. Tsippy was looking forward very much to having her wedding ceremony outside. The guests began to assemble on the lawn when it suddenly began to cloud over and thunder. Everyone rushed inside to the wedding chapel.

When the ceremony was over, the sun came out again. I heard that rain at a wedding is supposed to be lucky! Larry and Tsippy went back to live in California. Larry completed an eight-month course in graphic arts while Tsippy worked in a hospital in the Maternity Ward.

However, Larry was not feeling well. He was previously diagnosed with a duodenal ulcer. A recent endoscopy ruled out ulcers and a colonoscopy proved negative, Baruch Hashem! His stomach problem may be related to food allergies. When I was at the Wall in Jerusalem I prayed for Larry. I pray for a complete recovery so that he can use the talents that God gave him (His artwork is so colorful and inspiring and a sample of his work is the cover of this book!)

Not long before Larry and Tsippy got married there was a strange occurrence in Tsippy's apartment in Los Angeles. Both Larry and Tsippy witnessed it. It was daytime, a bright sunny day. Suddenly the couple saw their apartment turn pitch black for a few seconds. It then turned light as before. There was no eclipse or rainstorm to explain it.

We still don't know what this was about or if it was some sort of message. Perhaps the momentary darkness of the apartment is symbolic of Larry's illness and hopefully the light returning is a sign of a cure, God willing!

A WARNING

One day I received a call from my friend Hanna who now lives in Massachusetts.

She previously lived in my house as a tenant. Hanna has been known to have psychic powers at times. She told me the reason for her call was that she had a dream about Tsippy and she was concerned for her welfare. She asked me if Tsippy took walks, probably around the area where she works. She advised me to warn Tsippy that this walking could be very dangerous. Hanna did not know where Tsippy works or the fact that she takes walks. That evening I called Tsippy and discovered that she had just begun a walking regimen with a few of her friends that took place near the hospital where she works. She admitted that this area was not very safe and was known to harbor gangs! She then promised to alter her walking schedule. Her friends teased her about this, but; nevertheless, they also decided not to walk. Then one evening, it was mentioned on cable TV that the area in Los Angeles where Tsippy works was infested with women gangs and the problem was escalating. One evening, soon after that, Tsippy was preparing to leave work around 7 AM when the work shifts for the girls ended. This would have been at the time when the girls would have been walking in the parking lot if Hanna had not given them a warning. Tsippy remembered that she had to attend to something and told the girls she would be another ten minutes. They agreed to wait for her and remained inside the facility. Meanwhile, out in the parking lot, a gang war was beginning to unfold. Two women dressed like men were in a van and were chasing a man in a car.

They were armed with guns and were shooting haphazardly. They drove around the parking lot twice and bullets were ricocheting off parked cars. Eventually, they shot the man in the car. Blood was seen dripping from the car as he tried to drive through the hospital gates to enter the emergency room. When everything quieted down, Tsippy went to her car to go home and noticed the car parked next to hers had bullet holes! If the girls were walking in the parking lot for excercise, they could have been an easy target. I am sure Hanna has saved her life. But Hanna will tell you its not her, it comes from God!

EDWIN

FIGHTING FOR BREATH

My son, Edwin, was our third child. He was a beautiful baby, born on a Sabbath day. He was born through Caesarian Section as was his older brother Larry. He came into the world struggling for breath due to an excessive amount of anesthesia that was administered during surgery. He was immediately placed in a respirator. As soon as I was allowed to breast-feed him, he began to improve and was released from the hospital.

Once again, when Ed was six months old, he was fighting for his life. He contracted widespread pneumonia. Max had left on a business trip and I was left alone to handle this life-threatening situation. My pediatrician felt it would be more beneficial for the baby to remain at home and I agreed. He assembled a tent made up from a sheet over his crib and I ran the humidifier. Ed screamed practically all night, struggling to breathe, as I held him closely and prayed intensely for his life and also for the secret to good health, for our family was always sick. Miraculously, Ed recovered, thank God! After his bout with pneumonia, I was given health hints from some of my friends and began to read health books. I made vast changes in our family's diet and saw a remarkable change. Yes, God had answered my prayers, Baruch Hashem! The attacks of asthma that Ed experienced disappeared. In fact, at the age of 18, he received an award for 2nd place in his age group in the Long Island Marathon. He ran 26 miles in 3 hours, 15 minutes!

Ed grew up to be a religious person. He believes that God has a hand in what he does. I feel because of this, his life has been running fairly smoothly. Not to say that he does not have problems... we all do, but I believe that faith in God gives us strength to face obstacles as they come along, making life, in general, a far smoother course.

MEETING LAUREN

One of the major incidents in Ed's life was finding his soul mate. Ed is a quiet person who enjoys nature, hiking, running, and windsurfing. While he was at Stony Brook, he attended an art class. There was a pretty girl in the class who found him to be attractive and proceeded to set up his painting easel for him before he came to class. Her name was Lauren. There was a class assignment to visit the art galleries in New York City and Ed requested that she go with him and she did. Lauren and her family lived not far from the University and Lauren brought Ed home to meet her family. Ed lived on campus but Lauren went home every day to her family. They began dating and the relationship continued throughout their college days at Stony Brook. Ed discovered that Lauren was of the same level of observance in her Jewish background as he was; He was a Conservative Jew that ate kosher food and kept Shabbat. In our experience, we did not run into many Conservative Jews that were that observant. It was like finding a needle in a haystack!

Ed was always a bright student and graduated from Stony Brook with honors. He was preparing to go upstate to Rensselaer Polytechnic Institute for his graduate studies in engineering. I wondered about his long, four-year relationship with Lauren. I questioned Ed about his intentions and he said that he planned to marry Lauren after he was more established. He felt that he did not need to get Lauren an engagement ring, that they had a verbal understanding. "You are going upstate and leaving Lauren without a ring? Talk is cheap! Without a ring on her finger and you upstate, the commitment is a weak one." I nudged. The subject was not brought up again between Ed and myself.

That summer, after graduation, my gift to Ed was a trip to Israel for three weeks. His sister Sue and I accompanied him. Somewhere along the trip, we visited a diamond factory. As we were boarding the tour bus, Ed 'knocked my socks off' when he announced that he was going to get Lauren an engagement ring at the factory. Before he left for Israel, Ed asked Lauren what she would like him to bring back from Israel and she said "rocks". He gathered a few rocks off the beaches of Israel, bought a locally made stone necklace there and brought them back to the US. The stone necklace broke soon after he gave it to Lauren. Ed fixed it and presented it to her at the beach, slipping the engagement ring on to it while placing it around her neck. Lauren saw the ring and in disbelief questioned Ed – "Is this from a candy machine" thinking that it was probably one of Ed's usual pranks. When she looked at it more closely, she was stunned! They were married a year later. (While 'Ed'iting this story for errors, Ed noticed that it was the 14th anniversery of his and Lauren's engagement)!

RENSSELAER

Ed has related to me that his coming to Rensselaer as a graduate student was fated, just like meeting Lauren was.

While informing a graduate student in a lab at Stony Brook about his future options, the student told Ed that if he chose to go to Rensselaer, it would be a good choice because a Dr. Mayle taught there. This professor had a very good reputation in his field of engineering. On the way back from an unplanned trip to Buffalo, Ed had a brief opportunity to visit the Rensselaer campus, but only at 7AM in the morning, because his companion had to be back in Stony Brook for a test that afternoon. The department head informed Ed that he had applied after the time that most of the money had been set-aside for other applicants before him. There was only a small amount of funds left; to cover only one year for one more student, but Ed had good qualifications. He advised Ed to visit some of the professors that he might want to work with in his field of interest. Ed attempted to speak with three professors that he thought he might want to work under, not realizing that it was quite unusual for professors to be there at such an early hour. The first two were not in, but after standing outside of Dr. Mayle's office for a few moments, the Professor suddenly appeared. He had forgotten that this was the prestigious professor his friend had mentioned; only selecting the professors he wanted to see based on their research interests. Dr. Mayle was very courteous and he spoke to him about his research. He informed Ed about one of the experiments going on in his laboratory. Another strange thing about this meeting was that on the Friday before, the same topic as Dr. Mayle's experiment was on was discussed in class at Stony Brook. This helped Ed to understand better what he was explaining to him and perhaps made an impression on Dr. Mayle. Also, since Ed had been using a windsurfer, he was familiar with the phenomena of stall, which was one of the topics that Mayle had an interest in investigating. He later found out that Professor Malye also sailed. After the visit, Ed was soon notified that he received the stipend. It was a teaching-assistantship, which is the standard mode for most people entering the graduate program.

In the fall, when Ed came to RPI, the first day, he had to go to a teaching-assistant orientation. He got there early and did not know anyone there so he decided to go outside instead of standing in the hall waiting for a half hour. He looked for a sunny spot to sit which was a distance away from the building. He sat down next to the running track on the grass. The path that Dr. Mayle takes on the track is the standard route from his office to the laboratory, and he had unknowingly placed himself alongside this route. No one ever sits in the area that he sat in. (He noticed this over a period of three years). A figure was walking by along the track. He recognized him as Professor Mayle and greeted him. "Remember I saw you last spring? I was going to try to find you this week." He paused a moment to recall and then he remembered him when he mentioned that he had studied his project at Stony Brook recently. He sat down next to him on the grass. "I like a person who sits on the grass" he said. He asked whom Ed was going to be a teaching assistant for because he needed a research assistant himself. Later that week he signed him up to work for him as his research assistant, which was a much better break than teacher assisting. They hit it off very well together. He remembers a Stony Brook colleague relating how "you have to butter up the professors to get a break". Ironically, this position just seemed to fall in his lap through a strange set of circumstances; some will say coincidence. But Ed says he knows, better! He had a hand in it! You know who.....Baruch HaShem!

Ed did not realize at the time how far-reaching his fateful meeting with Professor Mayle was....

It was about eight months after Ed had received his doctorate degree in engineering. He had applied for jobs all over the country, Switzerland, and Israel but was unable to secure a position. He was beginning to feel down-in-the dumps, when the phone rang. It was a long-distance call from Israel from the Technion University in Haifa. (As I was editing the previous sentence for spelling and grammer, I took a double take when the word "long-distance" appeared as lonGodistance! I was puzzled how this could have happened, since I am a fairly good typist. Max reminded me that when I did an automatic change throughout the book, of changing "G-d" to "God", the computer picked up the "g-d" from long-distance and changed it to God! When I looked at this strange "error", the word "God" is in the middle of it as He surely was!) There were fellowship positions available, and Ed was informed that he was their first choice of applicants. It seems that the research he was doing at Rensselaer was similar to what they were working on in Israel. In fact, half of the project he was to work on, was going to be done at Rensselaer. It seems that the circumstances that led up to this was setting him up to work in Israel by Divine providence. However, he was told that he would not be needed till October of that year. (This was only January) It was quite a long stretch for a couple to wait, especially since he was unemployed since graduation. However, this was all that was available. At the time, they seemed to have no choice but to wait. A short while later, Professor Mayle phoned him and informed him that there was a fellowship position available immediately in Germany. I was quite upset. Anti-Semitism was said to be on the rise in Germany, besides the fact that I would have preferred to see him put his research efforts into Israel. Elsewhere in this book, I mention that I purchased a full set of Kabbalah books...the Zohar. When I purchased these books, I was told that they held special mystical powers. I always perused a few paragraphs a day from these books, but now I opened one of the books and prayed for Ed. The very next morning, at work I received a call from Ed. "What's up Ed?" I asked, thinking it must be something important to call me at work. "Mom, I'm going to be doing research in Israel at the Technion, after all!" Ed's post-doc was moved up to February, and he would be leaving for Israel in a few weeks!" I could hardly get the words out of my mouth to say "Mazel Tov!" as my eyes welled with tears of happiness, even though Ed and Lauren would be away from the family for several years.

HAIFA

Upon arriving in Israel, Ed and Lauren ran into a problem with accommodations. They were having trouble getting an unfurnished apartment that had a stove. Meanwhile, they had to pay a fee for their temporary housing and they were low on funds. (Ed would not start work till the following week.) I prayed that they would soon find a home. Friday morning of the first week they were in Israel, we received a call from them. They had found a furnished apartment that was "very pretty", with wallpaper, a balcony and a view of Mount Carmel, (where Ed had first mentioned on his first Israel trip that he intended to buy an engagement ring for Lauren) . They were situated on a hill about one mile from the Technion in Haifa. Just in time to enjoy their first Shabbat together in Israel!

Ed and Lauren spent three years in Israel. Life, of course, was not easy there. Lauren missed family very much, money was tight and safety was always an issue. But they were in the Holy Land! Lauren became pregnant. She gave birth to a baby boy who was named Yosef Yonah. So my first grandchild was a "sabra" (A native of Israel). I visited the family shortly after he was born. I missed seeing Yosef's changes growing up as a baby that first year. Just before Yosef's first birthday, they were planning to return to live in the United States. I had mixed feelings about their return. Of course, I missed them immensely, and was happy about finally being able to see them more frequently. However, since I am so "Zionist", I felt sad that they were leaving their "true home" since I believe that is where all the Jews belong. The giving of the land was God's promise to His people. I long so much to be there, but Max will not live there unless three out of five of our children settle there and now the only one that was there was coming home. Ed completed his fellowship in Israel and the family moved to Baltimore, Maryland. There Ed took a fellowship at Johns Hopkins University and they settled into a nice apartment development. Yosef now has a little sister, Sirelle Alizah. She is a beautiful child, Baruch Hashem!

BLACKBERRIES

Ed worked very hard at the lab, at Johns Hopkins, often coming home late. Sabbath was the only day on which he rested. He recounts the following message he received relating to his late hours. On Sabbath, when he had time to read, Ed came across a story about a father who had not been spending enough time with his son. The son arranged a trip with him to pick blackberries. The father enjoyed this trip very much. Years later during a period of depression, the memory of the blackberry picking brought joy again to him. It was ironic, because Ed had not been spending enough time with his family also. The morning after he read the story, his son Yosef was watching a children's program and blackberries were mentioned. To Ed this was a sign and he resolved to come home earlier from work to his family! (Also, the day Ed reviewed this story for accuracy, Ed heard Yosef mention to his cousins about how great it is to pick blackberries. They had done this as a family two years before and Ed had not realized that it had made such an impression on Yosef. Ed got the message again to spend more time with his family!)

FELICIA

A TOTAL ECLIPSE

Being an only child, I had a close relationship with my parents. I felt very responsible for them and loved them very much, although at times we would have disagreements. My mother was ill most of her life. She had rheumatic heart disease. After the birth of my third child, Eddie, she began deteriorating quickly. She could no longer enjoy outings with her grandchildren. The difficult breathing and pain outweighed the pleasure. Mom was visiting at our house in Rego Park one day and was feeling quite sick. I called an ambulance, which came for her at exactly the time of a total eclipse. As she was placed on the stretcher, the sky darkened ominously. The ride to the hospital under darkened skies was eerie and a sign to me of what was to come. After a brief hospital stay, she came to our home for a few weeks. The children had colds that made her susceptible in her weakened condition. She contracted pneumonia and wished to go to her home in the Bronx. After being home for a few days, and not feeling better, an ambulance was summoned for her again. That Monday morning, April 13, 1970, I received a call that my mother had passed away. She was buried the next day, which would have been her wedding anniversary. My parents would have been married 32 years.

A PREDICTION

The months that followed were difficult for me. I wanted very much for my mother's name to be carried on. I became pregnant although I was in a somewhat "risk" group due to bad varicose veins, repeated miscarriages and multiple Caesarians. I thank God, it proved however to be an uncomplicated pregnancy.

A few weeks before my due date, my daughter Sue, who was 9 years old at that time, announced with much certainty that this baby would be born August 1. August 1 came and there was no sign of labor. It was 5pm in the evening and I realized I needed bread from the bakery, which was quite a walking distance from the house. After I returned home, I had a nagging backache that would come and go. I ignored it, thinking it was just caused by carrying the weight of the baby. It became worse and by 8pm, I decided to call the doctor, ...just in case. I discovered he was on a trip upstate trying to get back to New York during a terrible thunderstorm. The bridge had broken there. I was told to go to the hospital immediately. He finally arrived at the hospital at 11pm and was quite annoyed at me for waiting so long to call. For Caesarians, it is quite imperative not to go into strong labor. However, everything was fine, Baruch Hashem! Felicia Dawn Malkiel entered this world at 11:58 pm, August 1, just as Sue had predicted! Just 2 more minutes and she would have been wrong!

My mother's name was Frieda, which in Yiddish means happiness. I did not want to name her exactly after my mother for the memory would hurt too much. I named her Felicia, which also means happy in Spanish and came close enough to sounding like Frieda. She must have known the meaning of her name for the nurses in the maternity ward could not get over the baby that was always smiling! As she grew up, people always commented on her happy disposition. I hope this makes up for all the crying and pain of her namesake.

That first year after my mother's death was still difficult for me. At the times when memories of my mother would overwhelm me, Felicia would begin crying and I would rush to attend to her, forgetting my grief.

MEETING KEITH

Felicia grew up to be an easy-going, quiet child. She was also quite intelligent. Upon entering Stony Brook University she was in the first Honors College Program ever offered at the University. She majored in biology and chemistry. During her years at Stony Brook, she too, like her brother Ed, met her spouse there.

Keith and Felicia were married the summer following Felicia's graduation from Stony Brook, on her birthday, August 1, 1993. (It just happened that that was the only date available for the hall, just like Ed' s wedding on his birthday too, that was also in August!) Keith is a fine young man, and I am very fortunate to have all of my children married to such wonderful mates, Baruch Hashem!

The evening before the wedding there was a rehearsal dinner at which the guests were invited to speak about the bride and groom if they wished to. I felt I had to share with everyone the way that both Felicia and Keith had come to a selfless decision concerning each other about their future. Keith had been offered a very good position in Chicago and Felicia was accepted by both Yale and Princeton for grad school. Felicia was willing to check out the University of Chicago and forego Yale or Princeton so that Keith could take his job offer. After visiting the school, Felicia preferred Princeton. Keith gave up his offer in order that Felicia could go on to Princeton so that he would have peace of mind about her safety. This meant that he would have to commute from Princeton to Manhattan each day to his old job. His unselfishness paid off, however. After commuting for six months, a job at Princeton practically "fell into his lap". One day as he got onto a late 11:30 train at Penn Station, he started up a conversation with the passenger next to him, since his destination was also Princeton. Not too many people that boarded the train were headed for Princeton. Ironically, this person was a friend of the owner of a computer consulting company that had been advertising for someone for the past six months! The company was located in Princeton! When Keith was job-hunting, he had been checking the local ads and had not checked the New York papers where this ad appeared. It just so happened that Keith had his resume in his briefcase at the time and handed it to the gentleman. It turned out that Keith was just the person they were looking for and he was hired! I believe God was repaying Keith for the sacrifice he made to Felicia.

A SABBATH VISITOR

When our large family was gathered at the Seder table one Passover, Keith announced that Felicia was pregnant. She had decided to give up a good job to stay home and take care of her baby. Benjamin Hillel was born on December 5, the second day of Chanukah. I was elated when Felicia advised us that their family would like to move in with us so that they could save up money to buy a house. When they moved in, everything seemed to be working out fine. The furniture in all the rooms just seemed to fit perfectly. On the first Shabbat we spent together, it was so beautiful and peaceful having the two families together. As I looked at the Shabbat candles, I noticed the wax running down one of them. It was in the shape of a woman. The following Shabbat the same thing happened! Strange as it may seem, I believe it was the soul of my Mom coming to visit her namesake, Felicia!

A SPIRITUAL CHANGE

Felicia is a quite observant Conservative Jewish woman, keeping kosher, observing Sabbath, attending services regularly, etc. However, Keith was not into it as much as his wife and was trying to please Felicia by attending services with her. He found it difficult to follow the service and it did not seem to hold his interest enough. One Yom Kippur Eve, he was not feeling well and had to remain home. As we were departing for the synagogue, he asked me what he could do to become inspired for this awesome holiday (The Day of Atonement). Rushing out the door, I told him I would have to "sleep on it". The next morning, he was still sick and I handed him a book "The Committed Life" by Rebbetzin Esther Jungreis. Felicia had purchased it and I had recently read it and found it to be very inspiring and easy reading. Well, he read the book and at one point, I thought we were going to have a Hassid in the family! He became very enthused and very willingly attends services. He learned to sing the prayers beautifully and studies Torah every week with a Rabbi. He even asked me to bring him back Tefillin from Israel when I visited. I am very proud of Keith and happy for him and his family! The message I received from this is that at any point, a person can change. Anything is possible!

GOING FORTH

After living with us for approximately two years Keith and Felicia bought a house in Greenlawn, 20 minutes away from us. When Felicia and Keith moved into their new home, the parsha from the Torah that is read in the synagogue for that week was Lech Lecha, which means in Hebrew "Go forth". It is the portion in the Bible in which God tells Abraham to go forth from his father's house, to leave his relatives and relocate to another land. I continually find that the Torah portion for the week has something in it that coincides with what is going on in our present-day lives. I believe it was the right time for the family to "Lech Lecha" (go forth) to become more independent, have more privacy, etc.,

The first few weeks when Felicia and Keith came to visit us for Shabbat dinner after they first moved into their home, the same thing happened with the candles. Only this time, there were what appeared to be wings on the woman! Could this represent Felicia flying the coop?

"FRUITFUL & MULTIPLY"

A short time after Felicia and Keith moved into their new home, Max and I were invited there for Sabbath dinner on Friday evening. At this dinner Keith and Felicia announced that they were expecting a second child, Baruch Hashem! The baby was expected around Rosh Hashana and Lauren and Ed expected their second child around Passover. This would be our sixth grandchild, which would exceed, by one, the five children that Max and I had. In Synagogue, the following morning, I was on cloud nine, thanking God for our blessings. Vayigash was the name of the Torah portion read that day. I noticed that our name, Malkiel, was mentioned in it (Malchiel was a grandson of Asher, of one of the twelve tribes of Israel). At the end of the parsha it was mentioned that Israel was "fruitful and multiplied greatly". The Haftorah portion that is read along with Vayigash (Ezekiel XXXVII, verses 15-28) also mentioned at the end of it that God would "establish and multiply" the Israelites. Here again, the Torah portion for the week locked in for me!

Felicia gave birth to her second son, Ilan Zachary, on August 10, 2002. When he was a few days old, it was noticed that he was somewhat jaundiced. If this condition did not clear up in a short time, he would have to be hospitalized for treatment. Also, a Jewish baby must be circumcised on the eighth day of birth, barring any physical complications. If he did not get better, the circumcision would have to be delayed. Of course, Felicia was distraught.

I immediately turned to my prayers for healing. Felicia informed me that late that morning when the doctor checked Ilan his jaundiced condition had improved, Baruch Hashem!

A PLANTING

I was in our backyard with my grandson Benjamin the other day when he excitedly spotted a group of leaves growing together in the hard earth. It was late February and it was the tulip bulbs sprouting that his mother had planted years ago when she was a child. I am sure that at the time of the planting, Felicia could not imagine that someday her son would find joy in her efforts. A person's actions can be far-reaching in time as well as distance.

MICHELLE

MESSAGE FROM A POEM

Several years after having our fourth child, Felicia, we were trying to come to some decision about having more children. Max felt that I was high-risk, with all the miscarriages, severe varicose veins, the possibility of being bed-ridden, etc. But, nevertheless, I still wanted another child, but was running scared. This would be my fourth Caesarian Section. Although my obstetrician did not forbid me outright, he did not think it was advisable.

Still, I had a nagging feeling. I prayed for advice. As I was standing at the window overlooking the patio in our Carlton St. home, my eyes fell upon a drawing, and poem upon the wall of my sons' room. Larry had received an award for the poem from the Reader's Digest Poetry Contest. The poem was called "Nature". What struck my eye was the sentence "And all this He has created".

Alongside the poem was a picture he had drawn of two large birds flying, followed by FIVE small ones. The one at the end looked smaller. I took this to be a sign...a message that God is the creator of everything and that the two large birds represented Max and myself. The five smaller birds were symbolic of our children. No matter what would happen, I felt God would help me through it.

I had no idea of the trials and dangerous situations that would ensue in following this course, but faith helped me through it all.

MOVING TO LONG ISLAND

I became pregnant and we realized we should move to a bigger house with more space for the kids. The suburbs seemed a better place for them to be closer to nature. Also, the fees for the religious school they were attending were rising each year. We bought a house in Syosset where we knew the public school system had a very high scholastic rating. Feeling nauseous and weak and having to pack for moving was overwhelming. But we finally made the move, along with my father and Max's mother, (a total of eight people).

I was into my third month of pregnancy. I was shopping one day at a local fruit-vegetable market with the children. As I was picking apples from the stand, I suddenly felt myself hemorrhaging. "No, I can't be losing this baby, please, God, No!" I pleaded. I foolishly thought I would be able to drive myself home with the children. I mumbled something to the women at the cash register and she very wisely called an ambulance. "Who will take my kids home? My husband returning from work won't know what happened." I worried. I was assured that it would be taken care of. It was. The Nassau County police have always been there for me when I needed them. They waited for my husband at the station with the children. An ambulance came for me immediately and I was taken to the local hospital. It was confirmed! I was having a miscarriage. The weeks that followed left me with an emptiness, even though I had four children that I loved immensely.

I became pregnant again and I vowed that this time, I would take it really easy during the first three months (the critical period for miscarriages to happen.) We were on edge until the third month passed. All was going well. I was into my sixth month during the month of August, when my neighbor, Dale and I, were taking one of the many walks down Burtis Lane that we loved to share. That morning I felt slight nagging contractions and I attributed this to the "Hicks" contractions that occur in the last months of pregnancy. On our walk, we picked apples that had fallen from an abandoned old apple tree. We returned home and I still had the "contractions" that were becoming annoying. Let's go to the beach this afternoon" I suggested to Dale "Maybe I'll feel better after I swim." We packed the car up with the kids and headed for Stehli Beach. I went swimming and when I came out I felt worse. I was beginning to worry. This is lasting too long. (Almost all day!). We decided that when I return home, I would call the doctor. He called me to his office immediately and upon examination, informed me that I was in labor! It came as a shock to me. It can't be, I thought. I am only in my sixth month! I was sent immediately to the hospital. A short time later a baby boy was born to me weighing only two pounds on August 11, 1976.

I was told his chances for survival were 50-50 and that if he did survive, he may have many physical problems. I prayed that God would do what is best. He survived only two hours. We were devastated! Some people do not understand that even if you have many children, the loss is still felt deeply.

ANOTHER TRY

The familiar empty feeling was there again. I guess I am stubborn, or a glutton for punishment. We decided to try again, although many arguments ensued from Max of how dangerous it could be, but I was persistent. An old friend of mine invited me to visit her in Massachusetts. Max did not go. I felt that if I became pregnant, I would not be able to see her for some time, so I took the three youngest with me, leaving Susie home with her dad. We stayed four days but upon my return trip home, I realized I was pregnant. A few weeks into the second month, I began hemorrhaging. My doctor advised me to take 3,000 mg. of Vitamin C. He said it strengthens weak capillaries, which I was prone to. It worked immediately! The bleeding stopped. The months passed. I did not go swimming at all, due to the fact that on the last pregnancy they discovered I had an infection that could have possibly come from swimming. September arrived and the Jewish Holidays were approaching. The baby was due November 6. I was getting very busy with shopping and holiday preparations, when upon examination, I was told that the cervix is weak and labor is beginning. I was sent straight to bed in my home to rest and wait, hoping contractions would cease. Thank God, they did. I did a lot of praying. I was still confined to bed. When Succoth arrived, several weeks later, I could not join the family downstairs in the Sukka. Trying to keep myself occupied, I wrote this poem to be placed in the Sukka:

Succoth

Succoth, the season of our Thanksgiving

A time of Harvest; a time of reliving

The past of our ancestors in this booth

A time for reminding us and our youth

Of our blessings that God has bestowed

Upon us bountifully his mercy has showed

It's a time for gladness, a time for joy

For all to participate, each girl and boy

To make this Sukka as nice as can be

And carry out His Mitzvoth joyfully.

75

A few weeks later, I was allowed to come downstairs. The week of my due date, I was able to drive for short distances. I have driven the path down Berry Hill Road a countless number of times, but now I was keenly aware of its beauty, seeing it as if it were for the first time; the beautiful, tall trees with blends of red, green, and yellow leaves, changing their wardrobe for the fall season. This is what heaven must be like, I thought. It is strange how we sometimes tend to appreciate things more when they are taken away from us for a time.

A CLOSE CALL

November 6, my due date arrived and I was grateful that I had reached this time with no further problems, but I was still quite nervous. So much had happened in the past. Each night I would limit my food for dinner because of the impending Caesarian Section, which requires an empty stomach before surgery. On the night of November 10th, I lost patience and decided to indulge in one of my favorite meals; potted tongue. After dinner, I felt quite sick. The meal came up and I realized I was in labor. I remember going to the hospital in more fear than I had ever experienced before with previous pregnancies. Perhaps it was a premonition. Of course, I was praying very hard and this kept me from falling apart. I was given a local anesthetic and I was able to witness something of what was going on. During the delivery, my doctor told me that there was some problem but I was not fully aware of what was happening. I was finally told that I had given birth to a 6lb. baby girl and that she was fine, Baruch Hashem! I remember the baby being brought to me as they washed her down in a tub alongside of me. I was overcome with joy!

However, I was later to learn that I had almost lost my life. The doctor informed me that scar tissue from previous pregnancies had rubbed against the bladder during contractions until the bladder burst. I thank God that a competent urologist was called in. He was at the right place at the right time. I was told that I had more stitches than a "patchwork quilt." I would have to remain in the hospital for about three weeks to recuperate, but I was assured that I would be all right. Fortunately, I had my cousin Marcia take the baby to her home till I healed. She already had her own young family to take care of but was very gracious about doing this great mitzvah for us. I miraculously curtailed my stay at the hospital from 3 weeks to 10 days, Baruch Hashem. I was drinking an herb tea known for quick healing. The nurses and doctors were amazed at my quick recovery.

I came home, very appropriately, on Thanksgiving Day. Marcia brought home baby Michelle to me. It was the best Thanksgiving Day for me ever. I was thankful for this fifth child, for my own life being saved, and being together with my dear family. The message of the five birds in Larry's painting had finally been confirmed for me.

We decided to name the baby Michelle (Michal in Hebrew) after my Aunt Minnie who was a very caring soul to whom I have dedicated a chapter to in this book.

11/11

Since Michelle was born on Armistice Day, 11/11/77, I have been told that those are special numbers. Not only was she born on the eleventh day, the eleventh month, but also she was my eleventh pregnancy. The combination of eleven seems to occur in her life at peculiar times. We remember her <u>eleventh</u> birthday particularly. There were <u>eleven </u>guests at her birthday party that day. I noticed the check I wrote out for the pizza for the party was No. <u>1111</u>. Our dog, Butch had been missing for several days and he returned on that birthday at <u>11:11</u> am. When I was at the supermarket that day getting last-minute groceries for the party, the register came to a total of; you guessed it <u>$11.11</u>!

As Michelle was growing up she showed a great interest in dancing. She took ballet up until she was 18 years old and was in a cultural arts program for dance in high school. Her achievements in both academics and dance were very good. Michelle's major was dance during her first year at Hunter College. However, there were too many distractions at school and she lost focus on her goals. This resulted in her leaving college. She taught Hebrew as a substitute teacher for a short time. She became a waitress and worked in several diners on Long Island. I did not think Michelle was living up to the great potential that she possessed. I had misgivings about her future and worried about her. I turned to my Bible (Chumash) and prayed for Michelle's guidance. As I completed reading, my eyes were raised to a family picture on the wall of Susan with her fine husband and handsome son. This served as a reminder to me of the miracle that God had performed for Susan; taking her out of danger and had blessed her with a beautiful family! My eyes then shifted a few yards away to the right atop the stereo. There stood a picture of Michelle, as a bridesmaid, at the age of 12 taken at her brother Ed's wedding. I kept looking back and forth at these two pictures and I realized this was my message! If God had been so merciful in Sue's case, He would again help me with Michelle. I just had to have faith! That Sabbath, the reading of the Book of Numbers was completed. At the end of each Book, we recite, Hazak, Hazak! V'Nit HaZe! This means "Strength, Strength, Let us strengthen one another!" The chanting of this verse helped to give me confidence for the future!

SEAN

Strength was surely needed as I watched Michelle go through a bad relationship. "Here we go again", I thought, for I remembered the troublesome times we had when Sue was dating. Michelle finally stopped seeing this person, and was feeling quite depressed. She then became friendly with

Sean Anderson, a tall, handsome, black man, who was a DJ at a club. Sean helped to ease her out of this rough period of time. He took her out and showered her with gifts. He seemed to really care about her. He tried to encourage her to use her creative talents in writing poetry. Besides being a caring person, Sean is very intelligent, studious and hardworking. He is a "Jack-of-all-Trades" having a nursing certification and experience as a chef. I find it a strange coincidence that my son Larry is married to a black woman who also has a certification as a nurse. (Reverse roles)

As time went on, Michelle and Sean's relationship grew. "Mom, he treats me better than any guy ever has!" she happily confided. "When you have that, you have it all!" I answered. Michelle made it known from the start that she would never give up her Jewish faith and the person she married would have to be Jewish. Ironically, in the past, Sean had not been content with his religious background and had been "searching" as he put it, for a different religion. From affiliation with our family, he was exposed to Judaism. He attended the services on the High Holy Days, went to the circumcision ceremony of my grandson, came to Shabbat dinners at our home and visited our Sukka. He decided to become Jewish and enrolled in a conversion class, which he completed with my Rabbi. He was converted to Judaism the following spring. Upon conversion, a convert has to choose a Hebrew name. He chose "Asher". Ironically, Asher is the name of the grandfather of Malkiel (our family name) in the Bible. Sean was not aware of this at the time. Asher means happy and prosperous. The "prosperous" connotation seems also to be prophetic as you will read about it in another chapter where Sean literally followed a dream that came to him and shows promise of becoming successful.

Sean secured a limousine to celebrate Michelle's 25th birthday. A group of her friends were invited also. Unknown to Michelle, Sean planned to present Michelle with an engagement ring while they were in the horse and buggy ride that goes through Central Park. It rained heavily that evening and so that plan was canceled. They proceeded to the Dangerfield Comedy Club. While they were seated, Sean suggested to Michelle that he wanted to go outside to the limo with her so that they could be alone for a few minutes, since they were with the group.

She agreed and got the surprise of her life when Sean presented her with the ring. When they went back into the club, the comedian was telling a joke about the relationship of a black man and a white Jewish woman! After that, he asked if anyone in the audience was holding a torch for someone. Sean called out that they had just become engaged. The comedian questioned Sean with "Let me guess. Is she Jewish?" When Sean confirmed it, the comedian responded with "You're kidding me!" The couple was called up on stage and questioned and the "black man-white Jewish girl" jokes continued. What timing!

Michelle called me from the limo shouting the good news!

Max and I were very happy.

Michelle and Sean had a June wedding on Lake Ronkonkoma. It was beautiful! All of our 5 children were married at last! There is a special Jewish ritual when the last child is married, of which part of it is, that the parents are placed on a chair and lifted and the guests dance around them! A scary, yet exhilarating experience! But then again, those two emotions can describe raising children, also! With faith in God and his teachings, however, it helped us to raise our children and reach this remarkable moment!

THE APARTMENT

Michelle and her husband, Sean were living in mid-Manhattan the first year of their marriage.

The rent for their apartment was getting increasingly more difficult for them to pay each month. They had 2 bedrooms, one of which was occupied by Sean's musical equipment. It was decided to relocate his equipment and move into a one-bedroom apartment to lower costs. Michelle began apartment hunting. She found something that appealed to her a few blocks from where they lived. She filled out an application and put deposit down on the apartment. This was mid-October and the apartment was available November 1. She gave her landlord the two-week notice. Later, much to their disappointment, the couple was denied the new apartment due to discrimination.

Now there were only two weeks left to secure another apartment and pack, for the apartment they were staying in was up for rent. When Michelle began her apartment search again, she ran into several problems. Because the couple worked as independent contractors, they could not prove their salary stable enough to pay the rent. Even if they were to secure Max and I as guarantors, Michelle informed us that we would not qualify. We were not considered to have enough income since we were retired, even though we owned our own home.

The days slipped by, getting closer to the dreaded November 1st and no apartment in sight! Michelle was a "basket case" and I was concerned that the couple could become homeless. As a last resort, they could move to us on Long Island, temporarily, but Sean had to be close to his work in Manhattan where many times he was required to go in at the drop of a hat.

I began to pray fervently that God would help them in their dilemma. A few days later, I received a call from Michelle who was screaming with excitement. There was a one-bedroom apartment available in her building several floors above theirs. The rent was more affordable for them than their present apartment. It had a better view of the city, and had a much better layout. Since they had already been paying rent on time in their present apartment, there was not a problem for them to be approved. To add to this miraculous situation, their present landlord informed them that they could stay one more month and use their security money to pay for that month's rent. Also, since the move was in the same building, moving costs would be much less!

As Max put it, "It is so amazing how everything fell into place, like a puzzle, when, before, there was a stumbling block at every turn and everything looked so bleak!" I truly believe that praying HARD can help! Baruch Hashem!

Chapter 3

MESSAGES FROM BEYOND

I believe the souls of our loved ones that have passed away are reaching out to us in different ways; that they are always with us and protecting and watching over us.

AUNT MINNIE

My earliest recollection of Aunt Minnie was when she turned my 7th birthday into a dream-come-true for a little girl. My parents, being sick and poor, could not indulge me with toys. I had one yearning; to own a doll carriage and be able to play with the other kids on the block without feeling left out. When my Aunt asked me what I wanted for my birthday, I was too shy to ask and felt it would be too expensive. She prodded me until I told her, not really expecting her to get it. She surprised me with the biggest, most beautiful doll carriage I had ever seen! It was almost big enough and nice enough to hold a real baby! You can imagine the neighborhood kids crowding around me eager to share my beautiful gift. Aunt Minnie had made my day!

Aunt Minnie had two children that she had to raise on her own. She went to work as a cook while her sister Gussie took care of her kids. She worked in the "Borscht Belt" hotels upstate in the summer and in the Miami Beach hotels in the winter. Whenever she visited our home, she would always give a gift of money or food to help us out. When I became old enough to write, she would ask me to write letters for her to her children which by then were grown up and living in Maryland and California. She seemed to resent them because they hardly ever answered her letters or communicated with her. She appreciated very much my writing letters for her and would often talk of how she was going to put me in her will. I did not seem to think the letter writing was a burden on me and told her that.

Time passed, I married, had children and received a call from her. She wanted to know if she could visit me before her planned trip to Florida, especially since she had never seen my children. At the time, I was pregnant and not feeling well and the house was a mess. I suggested to her that she visit me on her return from Florida; that I might be feeling better then. I lived to regret that decision!

As it happened, my mother was trying to discourage my Aunt from taking this trip. She felt that my Aunt was getting older and not feeling well and the hot weather in Florida might be too much for her. My Aunt insisted on going anyway.

One morning soon after her departure for Florida, I awoke feeling very depressed. I had just had a dream that my Aunt was swimming in the Florida waters and suddenly she was being taken out of the water on a stretcher over the white sands of the beach. I could not shake the feeling of great depression. Max tried to console me with "It's just a dream. Try to go back to sleep." I did and blocked almost everything completely out of my mind. That weekend, Max went to visit my mother in the Bronx. I did not go along, since I was not permitted to travel to ensure the keeping of the pregnancy. My mother informed Max that my Aunt had died by drowning in the Florida waters! The dream took place about the time of her death. My mother told Max not to tell me the bad news since it would upset me. About three weeks later he told me about it and I had difficulty recollecting the dream and then it all came back to me. Besides being in shock about her death, I had guilt feelings about not allowing her to visit and see my children when she wanted to. Since then, whenever anyone wants to visit me, they are always welcome; the message being "Don't put off for tomorrow what you can do today" for you do not know if that opportunity will ever present itself again!

I am sure that at the last moments of her life Aunt Minnie was trying to contact me. I am sure she felt close to me. Max thought that perhaps she felt bad that she did not include me in her will, but I feel that I owe HER a debt for being so generous to me and my family through the years. I felt the only way I could repay her was to name my child after her, in respect of the merciful, compassionate soul that she was! My fifth child is named Michelle, (Michal in Hebrew, the same as hers) in her memory.

Two strange, tragic incidents happened the year that followed Aunt Minnie's death. Her son Ben was shot to death during a robbery in his jewelry store in California. Shortly after, within the same year, her daughter Kaye died at the young age of 42 from a sudden heart attack. Well, hopefully Aunt Minnie is finally united with her family in Heaven. May God rest their souls!

IT'S LATER THAN YOU THINK

I awoke one morning seeing my mother's name in lights, similar to a movie marquee, with dots following it as if something were about to happen.

It appeared in this manner: F R I E D A .... I sat up in bed, waiting apprehensively for something to occur. Just then the clock radio came on and my mother's favorite song began to play with the lyrics: "Enjoy yourself, it's later than you think; the years go by as quickly as a wink".

Around that time, I had been preoccupied with worrying about something about which I cannot even recall. But I do remember acknowledging the above episode as a message from my mother who had recently passed away, warning me not to waste my time worrying, but to enjoy each moment of life. Thank you, Mom!

A WEDDING GIFT FROM BEYOND

The day before my daughter Sue and her new bridegroom, Howie, returned from their honeymoon, Max was looking through some papers and he came upon a note written on pretty white stationery that had a $10 gold piece taped to it. It was a note from my mother written at the time of Sue's birth telling us to save it for her and give it to Sue at the proper time and that Sue should hang on to it until it is taken by her own children. Mom managed not only to dance at Sue's wedding, (see chapter on angels) but she also was able to arrange to give her a gift at the proper time!

A CAREER MESSAGE

My daughter Michelle's husband, Sean, had a dream about his father that had passed away the previous year. In the dream, his father was urging him to pursue a career in music. Sean already had an associate degree in nursing, but did not want to continue working in this field. Sean always loved music. When he was a baby, he was told that when he cried all that had to be done was to turn on music for him and he calmed down immediately.

Sean experienced the dream several times. The fact that he had the dream again seemed to verify the message. In the Bible, Joseph also interpreted recurrent dreams concerning a future famine and it came to pass, thus saving the people. Shortly after, upon awakening from one of the dreams about his father, Sean saw an ad on television concerning an audio engineering course. It spiked his interest and he enrolled in the course. He showed great promise and his teacher supported his innovative ideas. Most important is the fact that Sean followed through and did not ignore the message of the dream! Through much hard work, determination and faith (he asked me to pray for him), he has been requested to write songs for a major company. Hopefully, Sean will realize his dream, and the Hebrew name of Asher which he chose upon his Jewish conversion, will be prophetic, for it means happy, and the tribe of Asher in biblical times was prosperous.

A SABBATH ANGEL

It was Friday evening in Los Angeles. Tsippy, my daughter-in-law, had just lit the Sabbath candles. In ushering in the Sabbath, it is customary to extend one's arms in a gathering motion before saying the prayer over the lit candles. I have heard it said that this helps to usher in the Sabbath angels of peace into the home. However, this Sabbath was not starting out very peaceful for the couple. My son Larry and his wife had been bickering about the lighting of the candles. Larry would experience asthma in the presence of the fumes from the candles. He preferred them not to be lit at all. Tsippy is a spiritual person, a convert to Judaism, and felt it an obligation to light the candles. Larry went into the bedroom when he heard the voice of his wife calling from the living room, "Hey babe, come here!" "Hey, babe?" thought Larry, 'I guess she's not mad at me anymore' he surmised. As he entered the living room, Tsippy directed him toward the yellow-green blank screen, the raster, which comes on before cable kicks in on the TV. "What do you see?" she asked. He was amazed to see an image on the screen that resembles a painting of my deceased mother (Larry's grandmother). This portrait was painted by Larry's sister Sue and hangs in my living room on Long Island. In disbelief, Larry touched the image lightly with his fingertip on the arm of the figure. This left a small indentation through the dust (shmutz as Larry calls it) on the screen. Even the arms of the image had short sleeves like that in the painting. Tsippy and Larry agreed that this looked like "grandma". This discovery brought a peaceful unity to them that evening. The following night, Larry examined the screen and to his surprise found only the dusty indentation that he had made previously with his finger. The image was gone! I believe when Tsippy lit the Sabbath candles, she ushered in the angelic soul of my mother that brought "Shalom Bayit" (Peace in the home) on Shabbat.

ALICE AND HER NIECE

Alice is an old friend of mine that came to live with us after her husband died. She related this story to me about her niece. She was quite concerned about her since she had not heard from her in a while and could not reach her. Her niece was going through a divorce. One day while Alice was at work and worrying about her, she heard a voice call to her. It was that of her deceased brother. "Don't worry. She is with us!" he informed her. Alice promptly called the family and discovered that her niece had committed suicide!

YARZEITS (DEATH ANNIVERSARIES)

MALKIEL YARZEIT

The first year after my mother-in-law passed away, I was holding a Siddur in my hand, which is a Hebrew-English prayer book. Each day, when possible, I would read a portion of the Chumash, (the Hebrew Bible) and a prayer from the Siddur. On this particular day, a small white piece of paper dropped from the Siddur. On it was written the Hebrew date of my father-in-law's yarzeit. Ironically, it corresponded with the exact date I found the note on. Subsequently, that evening, I reminded Max to light a candle for his father as is customary in our faith. When his mother was alive, she was very concerned about not forgetting to light a candle for her husband. It seemed to me that even though she had passed away she was still diligent in her message to us to remember her dear husband.

Just as I am editing this page, I realized that this is the exact evening of her Yarzeit, of blessed memory, and that Max almost forgot to light a candle for her. I just reminded him to do it (or was it really HER soul reminding him to do it through my working on this chapter?!!!)

YARZEIT IN THE SYNAGOGUE

George, the custodian in the synagogue where I worked related this happening to me:

He had just finished cleaning the sanctuary and had turned on the memorial lights for yarzeit for the week. (The lights are lit next to the names of the souls that have passed away marking the anniversary of their death.) George was working in the hallway with the back door of the sanctuary open to the kitchen. He had an eerie feeling that someone was looking at him. He turned to look back and saw a women's figure dart past the wall. He continued working thinking someone was in the sanctuary and he would surprise her by looking away and then turning quickly. When he looked up from his work, he saw the same figure again. He stopped what he was doing and walked to the front entrance of the synagogue, opened the door quickly and turned the lights on as fast as he could and saw no one. As he looked around, everything seemed to be in its place. He then shut the lights off. As he looked over toward the memorial board on the wall, he noticed one memorial light flickering. It belonged to a woman that had passed away. It was in the exact spot where he saw the figure. He walked over to the board, turned the bulb until it stopped flickering and it became a steady light. (The way it was supposed to be.) He walked back out and turned the lights off in the sanctuary and all was normal. Just a soul making sure her yarzeit was being observed properly?

A BABY-NAMING

Sirelle Alizah was born to Lauren and Ed on March 11, 2002. The baby's first name, Sirelle, was named after Lauren's maternal grandmother, Tsirel. The second name Aliza (Hebrew, meaning joy) was named after my mother, Freidel, which has the same meaning. Lauren's mother, Sharry, had been staying with her before the birth to help her. When Lauren went to the hospital in labor, Sharry lit a Yarzeit (death anniversary) candle for her father just before she left the house late that afternoon. Just one day later, I had to light a Yarzeit candle for my mother. The Friday of that week Max and I traveled to Baltimore to attend the baby naming. Sharry and I sat near each other in synagogue and heard the names of our mothers being called during the Torah reading as Sirelle Alizah was being named. Tears of great emotion streamed down both of our faces as we shared this beautiful experience. Right in front of us were two PINK tissue boxes (appropriately placed)! We laughed at this through our tears of joy. I thought it was awesome that Sirelle Alizah was born and named exactly between the two Yarzeit dates of both her great - grandparents!

THE YARZEITS OF MY PARENTS

I realized during the year of 1995 that two commemorations of mine would coincide; my 35th anniversary and the 9th anniversary of my father's death. The Hebrew calendar generally does not coincide with the Gregorian calendar from year to year. Therefore, the Yarzeit would be on a different date of the Gregorian calendar the following year. Of course, I had mixed feelings about celebrating my anniversary, which is a happy occasion, and having to light a candle that evening in memory of my father's death. Then it dawned on me how positive a situation this was all around. I remembered how my father had been instrumental in my meeting Max in the first place! Had he not arranged for us to meet, there would be no Anniversary to begin with! Thanks Dad!

When I am saying the Yarzeit prayer for my mother, I am reminded of how she transmitted the foundations of the Jewish faith to me. Without faith in God and His laws to give me a blueprint for my life, my life would have no meaning and direction. I also would not have the strength to pass through difficult times without faith in God. Thanks Mom!

There was one yarzeit for my Dad that I did not have a yarzeit candle to light. Instead I used a wide candle that I use in the Sukka. At one point while it was burning I could see that it would not be big enough to burn the full 24 hours. I lit another Sukka candle by touching the burning wick from the first one in order to continue the light. It made me realize the parallel of my father's past life in which he gave me life and taught me important values that I pass down to my children and grandchildren, thus keeping God's eternal light burning.

COUSIN GUSSIE

One of my favorite cousins was my cousin Gussie, who is now deceased. She had never married and had no sisters or brothers. Her parents died both within a few months of each other and she took it quite hard. Living alone did not help. I would call her from time to time. As a child, I would walk to her home in the Bronx, visiting her and my aunt and uncle, (her mother and father) quite often. My mother and hers were quite close as sisters in a remaining family of seven sisters and brothers. Since they were both the poorest of the family, they had a closer bond with each other. "When you have money, you have many friends" my mother would say. I shared many happy times with my cousin and Aunt and Uncle. She had a mixed-breed dog that I loved to play with. There was an old piano that my Aunt would allow me to play despite my mother's protest that I would ruin the tuning. My cousin also had a great sense of humor. Sometimes the two families went to Coney Island. I still remember seeing the awesome fireworks on the Fourth of July there. We were poor but we had fun! We were able to enjoy the simple things of life and appreciate them. Being that my mother gave birth to me late in life, I am a generation apart in age from my first cousins but the age gap never bothered me. After my Aunt and Uncle died, I tried to give my cousin support. During one phone conversation I had with her I accidentally learned that my Aunt and my mother shared the SAME yarzeit date, my mother dying several years after my aunt. It seemed to me that the close bond they shared in life had something to do with them dying on the same day of the Hebrew calendar.

Chapter 4
MESSAGES FROM THE BIBLE

Many times I have had experiences during the week that were closely related to the subject matter of the portions of the Bible that are read each week in the synagogue. During the synagogue services, the Five Books of Moses or the "Old Testament", as known to Christians, is divided into portions that are read each week in an annual or triennial cycle. I have heard a Rabbi say that when we study the Bible, God is *speaking to us* through the teachings contained therein; i.e., the Commandments, moralistic stories, etc. When we pray, *we are speaking to God!* The Rabbi's sermon for Sabbath mornings is usually based on the chapters assigned for that week. Recently I read that it is believed in Kabbalah (Jewish mysticism) that these different portions read each week from the beginning of Genesis through Deuteronomy offer us insight into the spiritual conditions occurring for each particular week of the year. These sections, (Parshot) when read during the corresponding time for the reading, are supposed to "plug you into the universe" during the week. I often find a parallel to what is happening in my life at the time I am reading the particular portion and am able to draw much wisdom as a result. However, if one does not connect with the Bible each day to receive these messages, it's comparative to the Lottery; if you're not in it, you can't win it! Following are some examples of my own personal experiences with connections to the weekly readings of the Torah.

LOST BEFORE SABBATH

I was leaving work at the Levittown synagogue one early Friday afternoon to prepare for Sabbath. On the way home, I stopped at the kosher butcher and then I stopped at a supermarket near my cousin Jill's house to get her flowers for Sabbath. Her legs had been paralyzed for almost a year since she had surgery for colon cancer. As I stood in line for the register, I realized my wallet was missing. I did not panic too much, for on several occasions before, I had been known to forgetfully leave it on the seat of my car. I left the flowers near the counter and rushed out to the car, but was quite shocked and disappointed not to have found it after a thorough search. I tried to retrace my steps and decided that I must have left it at the butcher shop. I decided to proceed to my cousin's house where I would drop off some food for them and could use the phone there to call the butcher. When I arrived at Jill's home, I called the butcher and was quite upset when I was told it was not there. I had my charge cards, driver's license and all the cash from a previously cashed paycheck in my wallet. Jill's son, Hank, tried to calm me down as I prepared to leave. I did not tell Jill, who was in another room, for I did not wish to upset her. Before I left, I told Hank that I did not believe the wallet was in the supermarket, but I would try it anyway. When I returned to the supermarket, my eyes scavenged the floor near where I had stood selecting flowers. There was nothing there. Since it was before Sabbath, I did not have much time left to prepare for Sabbath before sunset and I was quite uptight. However, even though I did not expect to find my wallet there, I decided to go to the Service Desk, which was on the other side of the large store, and there were people waiting on line, which took more time. Even if I had dropped the wallet in the supermarket, I reasoned, someone probably picked it up and walked away with it. "Was a black wallet found?" I asked the woman at the service desk. To my surprise she answered, "Yes" as I anxiously watched her retrieve it from a drawer. I then identified the contents. Everything was there! This was too good to be true! I would have a good Sabbath after all! I returned to the register counter where I had left the flowers for now I had money to pay for them. I was informed that when I left for the car to look for my wallet, I was being paged. The good soul that found it returned it to the Service Desk. I felt so elated and rushed to the car to bring the flowers to Jill. Upon returning to her home, Hank answered the door with a command to "Sit down for this! You won't believe it". Hank told me that when I left for the supermarket, he prayed so intensely that he broke into a sweat. His prayer was that I would find my wallet in the supermarket. Just as he completed the prayer, the phone rang and it was Max calling to tell him that the supermarket called him to notify him that a Rosalie Malkiel had left a wallet there! I gave the flowers to Jill and Hank had told her the story and we wished each other a good Shabbat and now it really was going to be so! The next morning in Shul, I noticed that the parsha for that week contained a passage on lost articles!

ON POLITICS

During a particular week, I was feeling rather depressed about observations I was making about politics entering facets of every-day life. A person's capabilities sometimes seemed to fall by the wayside in place of other factors when choosing or holding positions. On my job, I had seen situations where there was a double standard.

It filtered down to where I saw similar episodes occurring even where children were involved.

My daughter Michelle was in a ballet performance where the solo parts were given out on the days when she was not scheduled to have a class. The other girls of the same age with the same capabilities as Michelle had been with this teacher for many years. Michelle joined this ballet company a few years later, coming from another dance school. She seemed to always be pushed in the background.

The Rabbis sermon at this time was on politics in the Bible! He mentioned how frustrated Korah, Dathan and Abiram were to have Moses as their leader. They felt that they should be leading instead. But most important was the Rabbi's statement about being able to overlook being petty and keep in mind the big picture; the goal of what is intended to be accomplished. Sure enough, the ballet Michelle performed in was very beautiful and the part she had in it was necessary and contributed much to the overall performance. Actually, her attitude to it was mature. She was happy to do what she was doing. The first time she did not receive a part she wanted, she was very upset. I gave her a pep talk about each part being important. I had forgotten this. I was not listening to my own advice when I was getting upset about "politics" at my work place. I had to remember that I was there to do my job as well as I can in order to help the office carry on for as long as it will; regardless of the politics involved.

The message I received that particular morning from the Bible and from my Rabbi was that, yes, politics will be found almost everywhere, even in the Bible. However, our attitude toward it is what counts. There are times when we cannot let our own ego get in the way of the overall success of a project. We must acknowledge what is important in order to reach our worthy goals, with God's help.

ON PERSONAL INJURIES

After I broke my leg, severely, I became involved in a lawsuit. I had never sued anyone before in my life and I had mixed feelings about it. The week that we signed the retainer for the lawyer, the Parsha for the week from the Torah was Mishpatiim, which refers to laws pertaining to personal injury. That week, the sermon on the computer from the Internet, (since being handicapped, I was not able to attend synagogue services) pertained to the Talmudic rabbis' interpretation of this parsha which involved personal injury and the injured party's right to compensation for loss of use, pain and suffering, etc.

It could not have been better timing to confirm my feelings as to my rights in this situation.

"CROSSING THE BRIDGE"

My daughter Sue asked me when she gave birth to her first child, to come and be his "nanny" while she pursued getting a doctorate in biology. This would entail me traveling a minimum of 40 minutes each way, 5 days a week, to her apartment in the Bronx at Albert Einstein Medical College. It would also involve me crossing the Whitestone Bridge. I had an aversion to driving over bridges.

Well, I decided to go the Bronx, anyhow! How can a grandma refuse to take care of her grandchild, especially when I felt I was needed so much? Friends and relatives thought I was "crazy" to do this; that it would just be too much for me. Of course, I had apprehensions about driving over the bridge, driving in the dark, bad weather, bad traffic situations, etc. Just before I began this undertaking, there was a Parsha read during Sabbath services relating how God said that He would go before the Israelites and behind them to protect them on their journey as they were going through the desert. I kept this verse in mind when I finally began my trips to the Bronx. I always put classical music on the radio. As I went over the bridge, I had a peaceful feeling of being suspended in the "heavens" and was awed by the beauty of the bridge. I actually enjoyed driving over the bridge! I found that driving at night was relaxing with less traffic and the roads were lit up fairly well. In bad weather, the traffic was slow, which gave me a feeling of safety. All in all, it wasn't so bad and I had a beautiful, wonderful baby waiting for me at the end of my trip. Once again, the parsha helped me to work out my problems.

TOLL GATE #18

On one of the above-mentioned trips to baby-sit my grandson, I was driving toward the E-Z Pass tollbooth on the Whitestone Bridge to the Bronx. The traffic had been running smoothly that morning and I had my classical music on. I felt quite relaxed assuming that I would arrive at my daughter's apartment on time in just about ten minutes. The thought flashed across my mind how fortunate I was to be traveling back and forth this heavily- traveled route each day for a total of at least one and one-half hours and not be involved in a traffic accident. Perhaps it was a premonition of what was to come. Before I leave home, I always pray that God will bring me to my destination safely and back home and that I will not cause harm to anyone on my route. As I neared the tollbooth, I noticed an over-sized truck in front of me and I wondered how it was going to fit through the gate. As the truck kept going forward, I assumed it would make it through. From where I sat I could not be sure. Suddenly, I saw the truck backing up toward me slowly. By the time I honked my horn and started to reverse my car, the truck hit me. I just sat there, stunned. The driver of the truck came out to see if I was all right. Thank God, I was fine, just unnerved. He apologized profusely, admitting it was his fault and that he was unable to see me in his side-view mirror. A police officer came over to see if I was all right and issued the truck driver a summons for illegally backing up. I surveyed the damage done to my car and realized I could have been killed!

When something like this happens, it makes you realize how fragile life is. I am so grateful that God was watching over me. This episode reminded me of the message that I received from the Torah before I began undertaking these trips to the Bronx. The above-mentioned parsha contained an excerpt about God watching over the Israelites on their journey through the desert; that he would be before them and behind them. This gave me peace and confidence to drive. As I exited the tollgate the day of the accident, I noticed it was No. l8 (Chai) in Hebrew, which signifies life!

THE AVENGEMENT OF A SOUL

On a particular Sabbath morning, the parsha had to do with Cain killing Abel. That evening, we witnessed on television a psychic who was able to track down the murderer of an elderly couple. The psychic received a vision of what occurred the night of the murder. It turned out that the grandson was responsible. I find that this incident parallels the parsha we had read that morning. In the chapter, God calls to Cain in reference to Abel's death with... "His blood cries to me from the ground". I believe that the uneasy spirits of the couple "cried" to the psychic in order for this horrible murder to be avenged.

"HAMAS"

During this particular Shabbat service, I was reading the Hebrew in the Bible and looking over to the left side of the book for the English translation. We were reading about Noah and a Hebrew word caught my attention: "Hamas". The English translation for it was "violent". This word was used to describe the type of people living during the time of Noah. How strange, I thought, that this fit the description of the terrorist group "Hamas" that we have today. I brought this to the attention of my husband and cousin Hank sitting next to me. After we were through reading the Torah portion the Rabbi presented his sermon. As I am a "regular" in attending Shabbat services almost every Saturday, it is not uncommon to hear at times repetitious comments about the weekly Sedrah. The Bible is divided into 52 portions for the year beginning with Genesis, after the Jewish New Year begins, and continues through the year ending with Deuteronomy. At the start of the next New Year, the Torah readings start all over again with Genesis. Therefore, I was amazed to hear the Rabbi start his sermon with a comment about the word "Hamas" which I had never heard mentioned before. He referred to the story of Gilgamesh that takes place before bible times which denotes a great flood taking place due to the fact that there were too many people in the world. The Jewish text did not have a problem with the idea of over-population since "be fruitful and multiply" is the first commandment in the bible. God, of course, did have a problem with "hamas", the violence that existed at Noah's time and sent a flood. The Rabbi stressed the fact that to help overcome violent acts in the world we have laws that must be followed and enforced and it is up to each and every one of us to eliminate "Hamas". I do not think it is coincidental that I stumbled upon this word in the Torah and that the Rabbi picked up on it. I think it demonstrates how the Torah written thousands of years ago still applies in the world today. With prayer and vigilance to see that terrorist groups like Hamas and hate of any kind is not allowed to flourish, we will be able to save our world from another catastrophe!

DAY OF BIRTH-BENJAMIN

My "middle" daughter Felicia was very much pregnant and during her baby shower, close members of the family were marking the calendar with "guesses" as to her due date, which was "professionally" scheduled by her doctor to be December 7, 1999. Since I, myself, had delivered four of my children three weeks early and my daughter Sue also did, we were expecting her to deliver three weeks early also. The weeks went by and no baby! Although Felicia was quite thin, she had wide hips, unlike Sue and myself. I was thinking perhaps this baby had more room to grow because of those wide hips and that's why it was taking longer.

On December 4, on Shabbat, I was called up to the Torah and given a reading, which is called an Aliyah. During the reading of this aliyah, I heard the Hebrew words "Yom Huledet" which means day of birth. We were reading the parsha where Joseph is in prison and it is the Pharaoh's BIRTHDAY (Yom Huledet) and the Pharaoh calls Joseph out of the prison. "Yom Huledet" stayed in my mind and when I spoke to Felicia on the phone that evening, I greeted her with "Yom Huledet"! "Well", I said it was in the Torah today! Anything new?" "Not really" she answered and just about when I was about to hang up, she admitted, "Well, I didn't want to get you all excited, because I'm not sure if my water broke, because it is so slight". "That's it"! I exclaimed. After having five children myself, I knew. Within the hour, Felicia was admitted to the hospital and Benjamin Hillel was born on the second day of Chanuka.

In Jewish tradition, a baby's name is not used until they are officially named. For a boy, the name is given to him eight days after his birth at the time of his circumcision. Exactly, one week after I received the Aliyah about Yom Huledet, I was given an Aliyah again the following Sabbath. I was wondering how come this honor was reserved for me since I had come to services so late, and then I realized it was in honor of our 39th anniversary, which was that day. In the excitement of the birth of the baby, our anniversary seemed to take a "back seat". This time when I was called up to the Torah, I heard the name "Benjamin" mentioned during my aliyah. This was the portion of the Torah where Joseph meets with his long-lost brother Benjamin. I found this very significant, since I knew that the very next day my grandson would be named "Benjamin" at his bris!

ED'S RETURN

When my son Ed, his wife Lauren and Yosef, their son, were to return home from a three-year stay in Israel, Ed called with this message: The same person who had sung the prayers at Yosef's Pidyon Haben (a ceremonial redemption of the first-born son in the Jewish faith) when I visited them in Israel added these comments on the Parsha for that week just prior to their return. (Ed told me he was a Torah scholar). He pointed out that Jacob and Joseph made their fortune outside of Israel and eventually returned. This gave me a better feeling about the family leaving Israel.

Hopefully, they too will be able to make their fortune outside of Israel. God willing, my grandson, Yosef, who is a sabra (born in the land of Israel) will someday be able to return to his native land in peace together with all our family.

Hopefully, there will be peace in Israel so that all our people will be able to live in tranquility. I have heard it said that everyday is like 9/11 in Israel because of the suicide bombers. People off to work don't know if they or their loved ones will be there when they return! Actually, we do not know what place is safe anywhere in the world because of terrorists. We must all pray for peace for the entire world!

THE TALLIS

Our synagogue is egalitarian which means that a woman, as well as a man, may be chosen for an aliya (going up to the Torah and getting a reading of a portion of the Bible that is being read that Sabbath morning.) On this particular morning, I was given the seventh Aliya, which on that day happened to be about the tallit, which is worn to remind us of our covenant to follow the commandments. I found this very appropriate for I had just had a cast removed from my wrist that had been broken and I was able to raise this same hand to kiss the Torah with the Tallit as is the custom. I found this to be symbolic; the Torah portion coinciding with me again being able to participate in the services more completely since, thank God, my hand was healing, enabling me to be able to do more in the service of God!

A CONNECTING LINK

The Parsha of Shemot begins the book of Exodus. The word "shemot" in Hebrew means names. Exodus begins with the listing of the names of the children of Israel that went down into Egypt. These names are already listed in the preceding book of Genesis. The beginning verse of Exodus starts with "And the names............" There is a commentary on this peculiarity of starting a sentence, no less a whole book, with the word "And". It is said that this was done to show the continuity of the past generation bringing it forward to the next book. You cannot understand the present unless you remember the past.

A strange thing happened to me on a Sunday when I began to read the Shemot parhsat that was slotted for the coming Sabbath. That evening, I saw a movie about a writer. In it, the actor is arguing with his Professor about the use of the word "And" at the beginning of a sentence. He cited several famous writings that used "And" at the beginning of a sentence. This reminded me of the very same situation I had come across in the Parshat that morning! This incident reinforced in my mind the message that we must remember our ancestors, and our past. It is the link that teaches us to avoid the same mistakes in the present and to emulate the sages for a better future. It made me feel even more the importance of studying Torah!

FREEDOM

The youngest of our children, Michelle, who was 23 years old at the time, had been having an on-going relationship with a Greek Orthodox fellow for several years. John and his family were devout Christians. At the start of their relationship, they had agreed that they had to be casual because of their different religious backgrounds and beliefs. Of course, "casual" began to get serious. Michelle started feeling uncomfortable for she began to see the problems they would be facing. John was reluctant to convert to Judaism and Michelle would never convert to Christianity. The families on both sides were religious.

Each time Michelle tried to break up with John, he would return pleading with her. Meanwhile, I prayed daily that Michelle would have the strength to do the right thing. While I was visiting my daughter Susan in California, (she had just given birth to a baby girl) Michelle had a dream that she was leaving Egypt and swimming in the

Red Sea toward Israel. God was calling to her to leave and He parted the waters for her to escape. Upon awakening, she analyzed the dream as Egypt representing John. She realized that while she was in this relationship, she was likened to having the shackles of a slave around her, being in Egypt. Breaking her relationship would free her, which was symbolized by her swimming in the Red Sea toward freedom in Israel as her ancestors did thousands of years ago.

Upon hearing about this dream, I received a Torah message from the portion for that very same week. "Beshallach" describes the Israelites fleeing from the Egyptians and God parting the waters for them to save them. That Sabbath, I was still visiting Susan in California and attended a synagogue service. It was 'Sisterhood Sabbath' that week when women are called upon to participate in the services. A woman guest speaker who was a Conservative Rabbi took the podium. She spoke about the progress women have made in the

Jewish faith. She mentioned that although we must look at our past, there are circumstances in our personal life that we cannot go back to. In fact, to save ourselves, we must flee. She likened this to perhaps a job that wasn't working out, a bad relationship, etc. She stressed the fact that even though it might seem frightening to flee, going into "unknown" territory, we must have faith and do it, that God will part the waters for us to help us through our tough time! If this was not a message confirming a message, I don't know what is! Michelle did pay heed to it! This can be a message for anyone, for we all have periods when we are afraid to make changes for the better and need the help of God!

Shortly after, I watched a TV program where a boy was dreaming that his dead father was calling him to wake up during a fire. There really was a fire and in the dream his father was beckoning him to wake up and go to save his little brother in another room. He awoke and did save himself and his brother. At the end of the program, the emcee mentioned that if he had just dismissed the message as just a dream, they both would have died. He stated how important it is to listen to your messages! So, for Michelle just having the dream was not enough. She had to act on it and so she did! Of course, it was not easy, but in time, they went their separate ways.

CLEARING THE AIR

My son-in-law Keith, at the time of this writing, lived in my home with his family, which consists of my daughter Felicia and their son Benjamin. Keith was expecting his mother Lorie to visit us for about a week. She had already booked her plane tickets. A call was received from my daughter Sue who lived in California at the time. Her husband, Howie had just been accepted for a position at Stony Brook. They wanted him to come east with his family for about two weeks. This trip had a possibility of overlapping with that of Lorie's stay.

This involved some rethinking of which rooms the visiting relatives would be staying in. Keith suggested that the college would pay for Howie's hotel fees. I "over-reacted" as I was later told and became quite upset during this discussion, as I did not want members of my family to go to a hotel. I tried to control myself, but eventually I had an outburst. Later Felicia came down the stairs with Keith, ready to "talk it over". Keith was "big enough" to admit that he had spoken rashly in an effort to make his Mom's visit nice. This particular week we read in Kedoshim .... "Thou shall not hate thy brother in thy heart; thou shalt surely rebuke thy neighbor and not bear sin because of him." This is exactly what happened. If I had not addressed the misunderstanding, my unwarranted anger could have turned to undesirable feelings. Most important, the "rebuke" must be done in loving kindness, not in anger. Keith and I ended our discussion in a frame of love and respect for each other.

THE SPIES

This was to be my seventh trip to Israel. It was the summer of 2001 and it seemed quite a dangerous time to go. Suicide bombings were occurring, one of which killed about 20 teenagers in a Tel Aviv nightclub. I thought back to my previous trips and knew that it never seemed like a "safe" time to go, but we would return from these trips safely, Baruch Hashem. This time, however, there seemed to be more incidents occurring. There was a point, I was told, where all flights to Israel were canceled, except for El Al (the airline we were planning to take). At that time, I had people asking me if I had canceled our flight. Even my own family seemed concerned for us. Tourism in Israel was reported to be 50% down. This made us more determined to go! Israel needs us we felt and it seemed like only a small token in order to help the country. My Israeli friend, Limor, told me that everyday life went on as usual and she felt it was safe. We avoided going to the West Bank and "hot spots" like Hebron. While in Israel we felt quite safe, even going out at night in Jerusalem and Tel Aviv at 11pm. (Much safer than going to Manhattan or walking in Central Park!) The crime element except for terrorism is very low in Israel.

One of the tours we took was to Mt. Karkom in the desert. This mountain is believed to be, by an Italian archaeologist, the real Mt. Sinai according to stone markings and artifacts found. While we were there, I remained at the base of the mountain. I stayed near the jeep, waiting for the group to return, for I was unable to climb because of a back problem. I turned to read Shelach Lecha in my Chumash, which was the parsha for that week. It pertained to God sending representatives from the tribes of Israel to spy out the land of Canaan, which He promised to give to the children of Israel. The spies return reporting that the land "floweth with milk and honey" but related that there were giants there and they felt as "grasshoppers" in their sight thus spreading fear to the people about the land. God became angry at this attitude. During my trip I felt that Israel was more beautiful than ever (land of milk and honey) and I felt safe. The tour guide told me to go back to the US and tell everyone this. You guessed, it! I felt like one of the spies, but I brought back a good report telling everyone to visit and enjoy Israel as I did!

GLORIA

A temple member I met and would talk to during the Kiddush on Saturday related to me how after almost losing her life four times, she started thinking that someone up there must be watching over her. It was her birthday and the parsha this Sabbath was about B'tzalel, an artist. Gloria was an artist. The rabbi that Sabbath gave a sermon about artists and she told me that there was a special prayer in the Talmud that was read this week for artists. You couldn't convince her that this was coincidence. She had been through too much not to have faith and believe that everything has a purpose; a plan that is implemented by God according to the actions of man. Here again, I believe God is talking to us, through episodes that happen to us during our lifetime, but we are not all listening. How much better would the quality of life be if we listen to these messages.

Since this was written, sad to say, Gloria has passed on. But during her lifetime, she was a shining example of faith and her works of art and beliefs are inspiring.

LIVE YOUR LIFE

I am sure throughout life you have had to change your plans at times. It can sometimes be disappointing; especially if you have to cancel something you were looking forward to. Recently this happened to me, about some quite insignificant outing, but it left me feeling despondent. I opened my bible to read the portion for the week. It was "Vayyechi" that begins with "And Jacob lived"..... This was the chapter about Jacob's death, but the word "lived" and "his days" are mentioned with the commentary 'He lived every day, every moment counted.' These words reminded me to make the most of my day, even though plans had been changed. It also reminded me not to waste time, as every moment that God gives us is precious!

FROM STRENGTH TO STRENGTH

One Shabbat in early January 1996, I was given the honor in synagogue of tying the Torah together for the last portion of the reading of Genesis. When we complete reading one of the Five Books of Moses, it is marked by saying in Hebrew, "Hazak! Hazak!" (which means from strength to strength, let us strengthen one another) for completion of any undertaking is important. I found it very symbolic when I found out that Ed had just finished writing a paper for his post-doc in Israel. He had worked very hard on this paper and with his wife, Lauren's support and God's help he was able to complete his work. (and let us strengthen one another, Amen!)

On another Shabbat morning in the Temple, I received the seventh aliya to go up to the Torah for a reading. To my surprise, as I stood on the bima (alter), I realized that this aliya portion of the Torah also marked the reading of the end of Exodus, for the Rabbi and congregation began to chant "Hazak! Hazak!" It was difficult for me to read the rest of the blessing, for I was filled with emotion. This "ending" was synonymous with the ending of the work on my book. I recently began to prepare to send it to publishers! This was a message of hope to me and certainly gave me the strength that I needed!

As you can see, there are so many messages to be derived from the Bible that can improve our lives. So pick up this best seller (The Bible) and read it each day!

Chapter 5

ON HEALTH

HOW IT ALL BEGAN

When my third child, Ed, was six months old, he had widespread pneumonia. I remember that horrible night when his life hung in the balance as he struggled to breathe. I prayed fervently for his recovery as I held him close. I also prayed that God would help me to raise a healthy family. Up to that point, we had been continually sick with bronchitis, flu, etc. I was generally depressed for I was usually home with sick children. Baruch Hashem, Ed did survive that evening but the antibiotics affected his stomach. Recovery was very slow.

Around that time, I developed flu and my neighbor, Dottie, who was a Seventh Day Adventist, brought me over a large jar of carrot juice. I was not into health food at the time and people who were advocates were known as "health nuts". I drank the juice and immediately felt the aches and pains leaving my body! After that, Dottie gave me various books on health that I read with great

147

enthusiasm. I realized that what I thought was a healthy diet was not. I had another friend, Erika who was also health-minded. I often wondered why her child was never out of school sick while my children were. She introduced me to a book that advocated eating as much food in a raw state as possible. The book explained how our 'quick-fix' medications cover up illness and wear down the organs of the body. It brought to my attention that foods containing much sugar and salt could be toxic. After meals, I would reward my children with a treat of chips, pretzels, cookies, etc. not realizing I was feeding their bodies with toxins of salt and sugar thus depleting their immune system. I learned not to overcook proteins; that the more foods you eat raw, the healthier you will be, providing you can digest it. Dark green vegetables were always in our salad and we began to eat more fruit. We started to eat all whole grains; whole wheat bread, brown rice, etc., thereby, getting all the nutrition from the completeness of the grains. I realized that good health could be accomplished in simple ways. Most important, the more we eat the food the way God made it, without processing and overcooking, the more we obtain the vitamins, minerals and enzymes that He put there which our bodies require so desperately.

Over a period of time, I noticed a dramatic change in my health and that of my family. God had answered my prayer for good health!

I was also able to help my father, with God's help, when several years later, he came to live with us after the death of my mother. He arrived with kidney problems and an ulcer and was mildly diabetic. He smoked heavily. He was 80 years old at the time. The doctor advised him to stop smoking immediately or he would die shortly and he stopped "cold turkey". However, he still was not well. Erika advised me to "throw down the toilet" his antacid pills and other stomach medications and give him fresh baker's yeast as prescribed in one of the health books. I also revised his previous diet from "cake and coffee" for breakfast, and hot dogs, bagels, etc. to a bland diet, much to his loud disapproval. The yeast soothed his stomach and he started feeling better. He came to us a very sick man, but lived with us 16 years after that, till he was 96-1/2, in good health most of the time. That was miraculous! Baruch Hashem!

MIRACLE OF THE HONEY

At one point, when my father was 92 he became ill and had difficulty recovering. This did not seem like the usual attack that he would have from time to time when he would cheat on his diet. Those attacks would last a few days or a week with gradual improvement. This time he was not able to digest even the bland foods I offered him. The food seemed to "sit under the chest" he would say. He refused to see a doctor and became very thin. Some of my visiting friends feared he looked like a cancer patient and suggested I get him to a hospital. I asked the advise of a friend who was in the medical field and he felt that at this point he was too fragile to survive a hospital stay. When he did not get better, I became frightened and eventually resigned myself to the fact that he was "an old man" and this is the way it would have to be. At least he would remain at home with us where he wanted to be. An acquaintance of ours approached me about my father's condition. He was the son of a minister and he admonished me for "giving up on him". "You think he's too old. You have to pray harder." After that reprimand, I prayed with more confidence. I remember having the Bible open and a health book was lying next to it. In the past few months I had searched all of my health books for an answer, but to no avail. After reading the Bible, I glanced through the health book and it fell open to a section on honey. I had seen this chapter once before but had skipped over it thinking that honey would not be good for him because he was slightly diabetic. However, this time I read on and the phrase "honey is beneficial in kidney disease" caught my eye. I began administering the honey to him several times during the day in small amounts. The next day he passed, with much pain, many stones. I asked one of our Temple members who was a physician if it was possible to pass stones with raw honey and he confirmed it.

This episode reminded me of the situation in the Prophets where Elisha was asked to treat a bad skin condition of the King. He advised him to bathe in the Jordan River. This annoyed the King. How could such simple advice cure him? It did!

My father, after passing the stones, made a rapid recovery and lived four years after that in fairly good health till the age of 96. The honey had been in my closet all the time. In the past, I read the chapter on honey and had ignored it. Everything was in front of my eyes, but like Hagar in the Old Testament, when her son is dying of thirst, she does not see the well nearby until she prays and God "opens her eyes" to it! I needed more faith in God, which led me to the remedy, which was always there! Blessed be God!

THE DENTIST

We are told that the Torah deals with even the simplest facets of every-day life. When I was faced with the recommendation to have gum surgery, which is quite painful and expensive, I was quite upset. However, I did not want to "bother God" as my husband sometimes phrased it for seemingly mundane problems. Save it for the "big stuff", Max was bound to say. But this was "big" enough to upset me, so I prayed anyway.

I had been to four dentists and they all strongly recommended gum surgery. They suggested that if I did not follow this procedure, I would lose my teeth. As you see, I am also very stubborn. But I was afraid to totally ignore the advice of these professional people. I kept delaying my appointment.

The day after I prayed, I was in the health food store browsing around for some information that might help me. I asked the girl at the cashier for a book that might contain literature on gum surgery. A woman waiting on line overheard my conversation and showed me toward a book that had a whole chapter on gum disease. She also recommended me to a holistic dentist that treats these conditions without surgery.

This lady was an angel conveying a message that answered my prayer. After a few weeks of treatment, I could see a great improvement. The dentist also showed me a research report that stated that when gum surgery is performed, the problem often returns. The dentist's treatment was practical, not drastic, combined with holistic methods and it worked! The problem was treated at its source. I would do whatever was necessary to eliminate tarter forming around the gums. I had my teeth professionally cleaned every three months. I flossed every day and used a gentle electric toothbrush. I also took the enzyme supplement, Coenzyme Q10. This enzyme was studied in Japan with much success in gum disease. Trying to reduce my intake of sweets was another strategy. It is many years later, and I have all my teeth, except three wisdom teeth that were impacted! Most people lose their wisdom teeth, anyway, over time.

This episode confirmed my belief that if we come to Him, there is no problem too small or too big for God to undertake to help us with!

Chapter 6

ON GOD, TORAH AND SCIENCE

"THE BLOB"

Many years ago, when I lived in Rego Park, I remember having a "vision" of a "blob" of matter with small particles that became disengaged from the major object that would leave and come back to it in a pulsating type of pattern. When good was being done this phenomenon expanded and when evil pervaded, it would shrink. At that time I interpreted this, simply as a message about God and the universe. The small particles were his creatures going out and returning to the Greater Force. When good prevailed, I had the feeling that His glory was magnified to us. When evil pervaded, His magnificence shrunk from our presence as if He were hiding from us. I mentioned this "dream" that I had to an Orthodox Jewish man. He said that the concept that I envisioned has a parallel in Kabala.

Nothing disappears from the universe. It is impossible for anything to be removed from it. Everything that God created is necessary. What may appear to us as disappearance of matter only changes form. For example, when a leaf falls to the ground, it decays and turns into compost which later nourishes other forms of life. In this vein, I believe when the body dies, it also disintegrates but the "energy" of the soul returns to God. A Kabalistic belief is that, if necessary, the soul may return in a new human being's body to make corrections for a past life.

The fact that the universe is so vast and divided, seemingly into separate entities, makes it difficult for us to comprehend that everything is part of a whole. Each particle, no matter how minute is indispensable and has an effect on the universe. A butterfly flapping its wings in China may cause a storm in Florida. Small changes can cause big changes (Chaos Theory). How then must our every action have influence everywhere!

One of the sermons on the High Holy Days this year in my Temple was based on the "I" in the Torah. It really is the word for God. If we look in a "mirror" and try to visualize ourselves, (our souls) we are seeing God because we are an intricate part of Him. The Rabbi compared this to the waves in the ocean as each being ephemeral and unique in shape but still comprising the whole. This reminded me of my vision. We are all a part of God! This is a good reason for anyone with low self-esteem not to put themselves down; to have self-respect, realizing the awesomeness of God's creation. In the same vein, we also must not hurt each other psychologically or physically, for we are all divine.

My son Ed was standing in for his wife teaching Hebrew school and he was wondering what the subject matter should be. He also, had heard the sermon, in our Temple on the High Holy days, and he decided to use the same theme of the waves in the ocean. As he left school he wondered if he had reached any child at all with this philosophy. He related this to me on the phone the following week. I told him that we could not always know how we affect people in what we say or do immediately, if at all. I told him about a friend of mine who is a devout Catholic. She was quite upset about a big financial problem, and the worry led to her heart palpitating. She caught herself and later told me that she thought of me and said to herself "What would Rosalie say?" Where is your faith?" She calmed down and her heart stopped racing. "Ed, you don't know if, how, and when you will effect those children, but I am sure you will have reached at least one of them. " I assured him.

As Ed continued walking home from Hebrew school, he looked up at the clouded sky. To his amazement, the clouds were formed in a clear, thin ribbon, like waves in the ocean, but separate from each other, the beauty of which left him almost breathless. As he looked toward the east, in the distance, the clouds seemed to mesh together. It was somewhat similar, he explained, as to looking down at railroad ties, each having a space between them; as you look further down in the distance, the ties seem to get closer together. This sight was parallel to the message of the unity of the waves in the ocean that he had just conveyed to the children in Hebrew School. When he related his experience to a friend of his, his friend seemed cynical. "I always see stuff like that", he said. I reminded Ed of part of the definition of a miracle; when natural phenomena occur at a specific time and place. He had witnessed this right after teaching about the wholeness of the universe. It was as if God is confirming to him this concept. I see the clouds coming together in the east as a symbol of Jerusalem (Jews face east to Jerusalem when praying). The clouds coming together are to me a sign of the three religions that abide in Jerusalem; coming together to acknowledge the universality of one God over all people.

GOD-THE AUTHOR OF THE TORAH

Scholars have debated whether man wrote the Torah, perhaps even that several people wrote it at different times. I have always felt that if God did not Himself write this awesome document, it was certainly divinely inspired.

Recently I saw a TV program that demonstrated how scholars, mathematicians, and scientists have come across coded messages in the Torah. By using the computer and counting every 50 letters as the code system, the word "Torah" was spelled out in the first two books. In the last two books, Torah was spelled backwards. When the middle of the 5 books was decoded, it spelled the name of God in Hebrew. The word Torah, therefore, pointed to the center, (both forward and backward) to "God", thus demonstrating that God is the central source of the Torah. Also many predictions in past history could be found in coding the Torah, including references to Hitler, and the destruction of the World Trade Center.

Previously, I did not need proof that God wrote the Torah. I felt that it is a remarkable guide to a good way to live and that its contents came from

God in one way or another. After watching this program, I came away with the feeling that God dictated every single word of the Torah for man!

SCIENCE AND TORAH

Recently, I heard a lecture given by a physicist who had written several books on Judaism. I was fascinated to learn how scientific findings of late seem to coincide with Torah statements, and not conflict.

For example; the theory of the "Big Bang" helps explain that there was light before there was a sun for "Let there be light is mentioned in the Torah before it is stated that the sun was formed. Also, when God said, "Divide the light from the darkness," it may correspond to what was occurring in the theory of the "Big Bang".

He also spoke about evolution and Torah. When people talk about the universe and its' components occurring by chance, there are seemingly a myriad of perfectly balanced sequential events or forces that would have to take place. Chance would be impossible. Evolution may not be as random as Darwin theorized. When you see how intricately everything is composed; everything having its own pattern and purpose, it is difficult not to acknowledge that God guides evolution. I have read that some of the greatest scientists have acknowledged that there is a God, including Albert Einstein. It seems the more they delve into their research, the more awesome the universe becomes to them, making them realize the existence of a Creator.

Chapter 7:

ON ANGELS

In the Jewish faith, an angel is believed to be a messenger sent by God. The messenger can be of human form. We do not pray to angels since God is the creator of the entire universe and it is to Him that we come.

Now that we are in the new millennium there has been much in the media about the appearance of angels.

MAX'S GUARDIAN ANGEL

About 15 years ago, I had a vision that, at the time, had I told anyone outside of my family about it, they would have thought I should be committed to a psyche ward.

It was late one evening and I had been writing while sitting up in bed. My husband, Max was sleeping alongside of me, with his head against the headboard, while I was facing him on the opposite side of the bed. The bed lamp was on and as I happened to glance up, at the foot of the bed I saw a figure! It seemed to be that of a male, clothed in a white robe, with a hood, like that of a holy man. I saw only the profile. He seemed to be hovering over Max and within an instant he disappeared into the wall over the head of the bed. At that point in the wall, a white light appeared and vanished into the wall. I was quite shaken up about this at the time. I later told Max about it. He advised me, typical of him; not to worry. I was hoping that this was not a sign of impending bad health or that something disastrous was going to happen to him. The years went by and, I thank God that he was all right. What then was this all about? With so many people coming forth today with stories about angels, I look back on this and believe this was Max's angel watching over him, as through the years he has been saved several times from disasters. There were car accidents that he was involved in which he was unharmed. I also remember taking a walk with him one day and a thunderstorm hit the area. Max had a strong feeling that we should cross the street to the other side and he quickly pulled me over with him. In a split second after that, lightening struck the other side of the street that we had been walking on!

ANGELS AT A WEDDING

My daughter Sue was married on a Sunday afternoon in April. That same evening began the yarzeit (death anniversary) of my mother, God rest her soul. Several strange incidents occurred involving these episodes. A week before the wedding, Max and I visited my mother's grave. It is customary before a yarzeit to visit the grave of the deceased. Upon our arrival at the gravesite, there appeared next to the headstone, suspended in mid-air, a white object that resembled the shape of an angel. It might just have been a scrap of tissue, or something similar, but what was so awesome, besides the fact that it was shaped like an angel, was that it seemed to be held up by nothing and it was waving in the wind. Max and I stared at it, unbelievingly, trying to find out what was holding it up. Upon very close scrutiny, we

171

discovered a very thin, almost invisible thread that must have been a spider's web. The "angel" appeared to be "dancing" in the wind. I summed it up as a message from my mom telling me she would be dancing at Sue's wedding. A few weeks before, Hanna, my friend, was giving me Reiki treatment and during it, she said that the spirit of my mother appeared to her. She said that my mother would be sending a message in the future, at Sue's wedding. I discerned that message to be when, at the wedding, Hanna called me over to look at the candles at our table. There were two and the wax on them was melted down into the shape of angels, wings and all! When we looked at the other ten or more tables, the candles were melted straight down! I believe my parents were dancing at Sue's wedding! That evening when I went home, I lit the yarzeit candle for my mother's death anniversary with a wonderful feeling knowing in my heart that she had been able to share this great joy!

ANGELS OUTSIDE OF ISRAEL

I had mixed feelings about Ed, my son, and his family returning home from Israel. He spent three years there doing a post-doc in Engineering at the Technion in Haifa. His low salary and missing the family had a lot to do with their decision to return to the US. They were due to come home in a few weeks. During their stay in Israel, my first grandchild was born, a Sabra, (born in Israel) whose name is Yosef. Of course, I missed them immensely and missed changes in Yosef's growth as a baby. I was so much looking forward to their arrival. However, since I am so "Zionist", I still felt sad that they were leaving their "true home", since I believe that is where all Jews belong; the giving of the land was God's promise to His people. I long so much to be there, but Max will not live there unless three out of five of our children settle there and now the only one that was there was coming home.

As I was driving home from work one day thinking about their return, I was feeling despondent. I happened to look up at the sky and saw a large white cloud in the image of an angel, big wings and all, across the blue heavens. I could hardly believe my eyes, but realized that if I kept staring at this phenomenon, instead of watching the traffic, I would perhaps be up there very soon. To me, this apparition was a message that God would protect them wherever they would be.

Since Ed has been in the States, I am sure the angels *were* watching over him! One March day while he was windsurfing, he had an equipment problem and was blown off shore. After hours in the water, he managed to get to a shore and in a near hypothermic state had to search for shelter in a fenced-off region of unexploded ordnance. In the end, his windsurfer was lost but he was saved!

A GUIDE THROUGH THE RAIN

During Ed's experiment on a submersible, his wife, Lauren and their son, Yosef, came to visit us on Long Island. When Lauren heard that Ed's experiment was done and that he was going home, she headed home to Baltimore also. While on the highway, it began to rain heavily, and it reminded her of Ed being underwater. Driving visibility was not good. Suddenly a Ryder truck, just like the one Ed used to take his equipment to Boston, appeared in front of Lauren's car. It remained in front of her for most of the trip. "Look Yosef, a truck just like Daddy's!" Following this truck, made it easier for Lauren to see and it was a comforting reminder of Ed. (An angel leading the way?)

ANGELS IN ISRAEL

After I retired, Max and I decided to take a trip to Israel again in the year 2001. Even though it seemed to be a very dangerous time to go, we always felt that Israel needed our support. As I was watching the news one evening about Israel, I admit I, too, was becoming concerned.

Soon after, one evening, my son-in-law, Keith had just come home from a Torah study session. He showed me a tiny little prayer book that his Israeli co-worker had given him as a gift from her recent return from Israel. The prayer on the cover was the "Traveler's Prayer" with references to God sending an angel "before you to protect you on the way". My daughter, Felicia, picked up our own standard prayer book to find a translation and the book opened up to a prayer that begins "So may it be His will...". The Traveler's Prayer begins the same way. The next morning, when I did my daily prayer and Torah study, the page in the Zohar was open to Page 222. I noticed that this was the same page as the Travelers Prayer that was left open in the Siddur from the night before.

I believe that these were signs that God *would* be sending His angels to watch over us on the trip and not to fear. The trip proved to be safe and wonderful, Baruch Hashem! During those several weeks, there was a cease-fire that seemed to be working for the entire period of time we were there!

ANGELS ALL AROUND

The first few weeks of December 2000 involved a strange series of episodes for our family. On December 5, which was my grandson Benjamin's birthday, he went into a seizure. My daughter Felicia was home alone with Benjamin at our house and called 911. The ambulance came immediately and oxygen was administered to Benjamin in our driveway. When he arrived at the hospital, he was given blood tests. It seemed he had a high fever, either from the hepatitis shot he was given the day before or from a virus. A high fever could cause a child to convulse. He recovered and seemed fine, Baruch Hashem! I later found out that at approximately the time of his seizure, my first cousin, Sol had passed away. Another first cousin, Sam that lived in Florida had also died about that time, God rest their souls. Sol was to be buried the following Sunday which coincided with an unveiling that we had previously planned for my other first cousin, Jill, God rest her soul (Hank's mother). The cousin's graves were only a few feet away from each other. While we were parked, waiting for the funeral car to arrive with the rest of my cousins, Max moved our car higher up on the grass away from the road, because he said he had a dream the night before; something about the side of the car door being smashed. After the burial, we drove to the house of Shiva, to pay our respects to the immediate family of mourners, in Franklin Square. On our return home from there, Max and I decided to have Hank (Jill's son) drive us home in our car since Max's night vision is not too good. It was a rainy night and we were not too sure of our direction. Max was sitting in the passenger's seat in the front and I was in the back. We came to a large intersection and Hank proceeded to make a left turn. Max yelled out to him "Stop!", but Hank continued turning. I suddenly saw a truck coming toward my window and felt the impact. I was stunned, but Baruch Hashem, I was unharmed as were Hank and Max. The truck had immediately left the scene. Several witnesses saw the truck speed away, but were unable to get the license number. The car door where I was sitting was damaged considerably. Max had dreamt about the side of the car being smashed! It was miraculous that we were saved. Two policemen arrived on the scene. In Max' dream, he saw two policemen both with blond hair, one whose name was Mike. This also paralleled Max's dream!

During that week, in my office in the synagogue where I worked, I had been typing up a 9-page booklet of information on funerals, unveilings, etc. that the Rabbi had given me to send out to the Congregation. It was almost as if it was a premonition of what was to come, for after the two funerals of my cousin in one week, the Rabbi's mother-in law passed away. (They say things happen in threes). That Friday afternoon, I was busy printing up announcement cards to inform the Congregation of this loss and the location of where the Shiva was to be held. It was imperative that I get the cards printed early that afternoon so that they could arrive on time to let people know when and where to pay a Shiva call. My hours were to be until 2pm so that I could get home and prepare for Shabbat. It was December and sundown is at approximately 4:30pm, which does not allow too much time to cook, clean, etc. before that time. It is very important for me to be able to make Shabbat on time for it is one of the Ten Commandments to keep the Sabbath. As you would have it, the printer jammed several times, causing much chaos. My husband, Max came in the office to drive me home, as I had no car available because of the accident. Instead, I sat him down to help me handwrite some of the cards that got messed up in the printer. While he was doing that, I typed up the Yarzeit (Death)

Anniversary and Get-Well lists that are read off at the Sabbath services, which were also necessary to have completed before I left. When I attempted to print the lists, which have a total of about 50 or more names, the other printer (Laser) did not function. I turned to Max and when he saw all the wires and knew it was computer related, he became helpless even though he is an engineer. For some reason, he has an aversion to computers except when he checks the stock market on-line! I looked at the clock. It was already 2:15pm. I was beginning to lose it! "God, what do you want from me!" I cried. At just that moment, the Rabbi walked in to get something he forgot. It was unusual for him to be there at this time. He saw my distressed look and tried to sort the wires out and discovered it was a loose connection. Once again, an angel (or a messenger) was there at the right time!

Chapter 8

TENANTS

While living in our home in Syosset, we were privileged several times to have people come to us looking for a place to live. In all these circumstances, we were not looking for tenants. They came to us. By taking them in, our lives were enhanced. The following stories will illustrate this.

Several times in my life, I have been blessed by following the commandment, "love the stranger" and twice it was through a Temple (a House of God) that this occurred.

LIMOR

The first time, I was working as a secretary in a Synagogue on the North Shore. The time was just before the High Holy Days of Rosh Hashana and Yom Kippur. A young woman came into my office asking for a place to stay with a Jewish family over the Holidays. She explained that she was an au pair from Israel and was working for a Non-Jewish family and felt that being in a Jewish atmosphere over the Holidays would ease her of being homesick. I suggested to her that she come home to our family. I was told later that I must be crazy to take someone "off the street", not knowing much about her background. I guess my gut feeling about this woman was that she was "okay" and the desire to help her, since she was away from home, overcame my fears. She spent the Holidays with us and we all enjoyed our guest and became good friends.

After a while, it seemed that she was not getting along with the people she was working for due to cultural and religious background differences. Subsequently, she was fired, with no place to go, except back to Israel and she did not seem ready for that yet. I offered her to stay with our family until she became settled with another job. It was several months before she found work and before we knew it, the Holiday of Passover was approaching. It is a custom to clean the house from top to bottom as thoroughly as possible (like Spring cleaning) before Passover. However, the cleaning has a spiritual undertow to it, similar to the cleansing of one's soul by eliminating all forms of chametz (bread) in order to keep the commandment in the Torah (Old Testament) that no form of leaven should be seen within the borders of our home. During this period of cleansing, Limor was like an angel sent from heaven. Although I protested, she insisted on working very hard to help in this project, and being that I went to work during the day, this was a great help. The house never sparkled so much on Passover as it did that year.

Limor is a very honest person and sometimes she could be very blunt to the point of offending people unwittingly. This seems to be a trait among Israelis. I guess you could compare this to the Sabra plant in Israel. It is a "prickly pear" rough on the outside and sweet and soft on the inside. Israeli-born people are called "Sabras" because of their tough exterior and Limor fit into this pattern. But I knew of her soft, sweet personality beneath. Limor eventually got a job in Flushing in a food place behind the counter. She moved to a friend's place and became emotionally involved with an Israeli. I believe that part of the reason for her trip was to meet someone in America and get married. However, this man seemed to cause her much heartache. "Drop him!" I advised her. "You're too good for him and you are young and will meet someone wonderful whom you deserve". I don't think she believed me, but in time the bad relationship was broken.

Later she returned home to Israel to her large family. Ironically, right "in her own back yard", she met a distant cousin at a party and they hit it off! She became engaged and they planned to be married that October. I was invited to the wedding but could not make it because I had just visited Israel a few months before with Michelle and Max. When I was there on that trip, Limor did not know what to do for me in appreciation. I met her beautiful family of 7 sisters and brothers and her parents. They knew me as Limor's second mother in the US. We stayed only overnight at their Moshav as we were on a tour of Israel. I met Avi, her wonderful fiancé as I had once predicted that she would meet.

Whenever we visit Israel, we are picked up at the airport by Limor and they bring us back to the airport on our return. We are always invited to stay at their home and we are treated like family. I know and have been proven many times that Limor and her family would do anything for me and anyone related to me. Whenever I visit Israel I know that I have friends always willing to help. By doing a mitzvah many years ago, by loving the stranger, I have been blessed many times over!

HANNA

It was the second time in my life that I had the opportunity to truly fulfill the commandment of "love the stranger" which is found in the Old Testament. As with Limor, I met Hanna also in a synagogue where I worked; only this time it was in Levittown.

One day a woman came to my office seeking employment and a place to live. She placed her ad on our bulletin board. A few weeks later upon her return to the synagogue, she was quite upset because she had not received a response and she could not find her ad on the board. One of the officers of the Temple informed me that it was not a good idea to post ads from people "off the street" as the Temple could be held responsible for any problem that may arise. I left Hanna standing at the board while I went to the other side of the building where the Temple ran a day- care facility. I thought perhaps someone there would have some suggestions to help her. Upon my return, I found Hanna crying. She informed me that the very next day she was expected to leave her present living quarters. She had been staying temporarily with a family that now needed their space and privacy and she was unemployed. I put my arms around her and tried to calm her down. I was thinking that I have a big house with most of my children gone. My husband was about to retire without a pension and we had discussed that someday we might rent out to someone, but not until the need would arise. We had bad experiences with rentals in Rego Park and this would be a last resort. "I might have a room for you to stay temporarily" I heard myself saying. I know that many people would think that I was crazy taking the risk by not knowing much about the person, but as with Limor, I had a good feeling about her and took the chance. Hanna came home with me from work and I showed her Ed's old room for he was now living in Israel with his wife. She seemed satisfied but was concerned about what my husband's reaction would be. I assured Hanna that it would be all right. When Max returned from work, Hanna asked him if he would consider her renting the room and his response was "If its all right with my wife, its all right with me." Moments like that made me love Max even more than I thought possible.

Time passed and Hanna proved to be a great blessing to us in many ways.

In Russia, she was a biologist. She worked as a Lab Doctor and has a medical background with many degrees. She is very knowledgeable and intelligent. She also has certificates in Reiki treatment and reflexology and many times saved the day for me when I had severe back pain. When I had surgery on my leg to remove a pin that was put there when I broke it, she was there for me. She helped with the pain and healing by her treatment. Hanna has a terrific sense of humor combined with her beautiful Russian accent, which she despises. She is a great cook. She is a concerned, very helpful person. Sadly, however, she has many problems. She came here with her husband and two young children approximately 23 years ago. They settled in Massachusetts where she worked in a hospital. In 1992 she became divorced and has been left with the remnants of horrible, unjust court decisions, which left her homeless and has affected her health. Her husband was given custody of the children even though she was beaten up by him and has pictures to prove it. She was staying in New York trying to rectify the situations from a distance so that she would not be harmed and be able to continue a normal life. I pray each day that her problems be resolved for her good and that her health be improved. Such a good soul deserves a good life and I believe that God will help her.

When I took Hanna in, the mitzvah that I did was returned to us many times over!

Hanna returned to the Boston area in the fall of 1997 to care for her sister who had broken her shoulder and ankle. The following spring, I again fell and this time, I broke my right wrist, disabling me from my job and driving.

(I am right-handed.) Immediately, Hanna boarded a bus to New York to come to help me heal by giving me Reikki treatment. I felt that she was an angel sent by God. Six months had passed since she left and it was so good to see her again.

During her stay, however, I am ashamed to say that partly because my pride got in the way, we became involved in a terrible argument. In the past, I had been helping her to write letters involving her divorce case. This took much of my spare time for I was working during the day. During a conversation, it seemed to me that she was not impressed with my writing. She quickly apologized, but I was slow to pick up on it, as I was hurt. This hesitation set the ball rolling for a full-fledged disagreement for, by the time I did accept her apology, it was too late. Hanna was lying in her room with a severe migraine headache and was quite upset with me. I felt that I had undone all the good that I had strived for in the past. When Hanna was not feeling well, I would try to restore her health through massage and diet. The aggravation I caused may have triggered her migraine. That weekend we were all going to visit my son Ed and his family in Maryland. While we were riding in the car, I wrote Hanna a long poem trying to express my regret. She seemed to reluctantly accept it. After the trip to Maryland, she returned to Boston. On reaching Boston, she called me to inform me that her sister had broken both her hands! Unbelievable! It seemed like she was forever going back and forth between my home and her sister's to help heal broken bones! An angel of mercy, and I had upset her! After she was gone, I kept receiving messages wherever I turned which I felt applied to my behavior with Hanna. At the conclusion of the Shabbat service, the Rabbi mentioned something about not letting pride and dissension keep us apart. Also, I noticed in the prayer book a reference to the effect that if we are insulted, we are to keep silent with the premise that if we leave it in God's hands, He would help us deal with it. Also, in my Kabbalah magazine for that month, there was an article on humility. It had a quote from the great Kabbalist, Rabbi Chaim Luzatto: "The essence of humility is in a person's not attaching importance to himself for any reason whatsoever. This trait is the opposite of pride." In Hanna's case, I had let pride about my writing get in the way, which, of course, caused much negativity. The lesson that I learned from these messages is that I had let my ego get in the way of a beautiful friendship; causing all the good things I had been striving for to help her with her health, to be destroyed in an instant. I prayed that the scars will be completely healed and that in the future, God will help me to restrict my ego thus enabling me to be a better person. As time passed, I am sure that our spat was forgotten and Hanna came from Boston to Michelle's wedding with her sister and niece. Recently, her health is not good and I pray for her complete recovery.

ALICE

I first met Alice at the school bus stop years ago when I was getting my youngest daughter,

Michelle, off to school. Alice, at the time, was doing child-care for a neighborhood family and was also awaiting the school bus for the children. She was a tiny, fragile-looking wisp of a woman, with fair skin, fine features and bright blue eyes. I came to learn that beneath that "fragile" look was an amazing strength for one day she helped to physically board a very unruly child onto a school-bound vehicle. This was not an easy feat especially for an older woman like herself. We soon became friends. I learned that her husband was ill. She would visit him quite often in the VA hospital. When he passed away she was left living alone in her home in Syosset. They never had children. She had a mother that lived alone upstate that she would occasionally visit that was almost 100 years old. Alice herself was then in her eighties.

Once in a while, Alice would come to join us for dinner. Alice loved to walk and if I didn't pick her up in time with the car, there she was on my doorstep in all kinds of weather, her trek being at least a mile. There was a spell where I would drop her off and pick her up at the school at night where she was taking a typing course. On one of those evenings, my synagogue held a dinner at which they would present a yearly "Good Neighbor" award. The name of the person receiving the award was not divulged, not even to the recipient till the presentation was made after the dinner. That evening I nervously kept looking at my watch as it was nearing 9 o'clock when I would have to pick up Alice at the school. I felt it would be impolite to leave before the presentation was made, but I was concerned about Alice. A congregant begged me to stay just a little while longer. I felt I could no longer wait and finally got up to leave when much to my surprise I heard my name called. When I went up to receive the "Good Neighbor Award", I was asked why I was rushing out the door and I had to explain that I was on my way to help a neighbor get home.

Alice was contemplating selling her house. I was concerned about her living alone and mentioned to her that in the future she could rent our mother-daughter apartment if she liked. However, she sold her house and went to live with a friend.

When I went to vote, I would meet her working on the Election Board and would invite her to dinner. Sometimes I would meet her walking in town and we would arrange for her to come to a Shabbat dinner. For a while, I did not see her and learned that she had a stroke. However, she was a 'tough cookie' and with God's help she recovered with minor disability and still would walk miles around town no matter what the weather. She felt it helped her circulation and I am sure she was right.

One Sunday morning, the doorbell rang. It was Alice. She wanted to know if she could rent a room from us for a few months. The woman she was living with had died and the family was selling the house. Alice seemed distraught. Her mother had passed away upstate. The house upstate was in need of repair and Alice was contemplating moving there when the repairs were accomplished. I went to check with my daughter Felicia and son-in-law who were living in our home at the time if they wouldn't mind. Since Alice would be taking the mother-daughter apartment below them, they saw no conflict. When I questioned Max about it, he also approved. There is a verse in the Torah that says, "Ye shall not afflict any widow". I don't think I had any misgivings about taking Alice in, but if I did, that verse would have been the determining factor. As I am typing this, a strange thing happened. I went to look up the verse in the Pentateuch to get the exact wording. The book has over 1,000 pages and it just happened to open up to this particular verse!

I also realize that by doing the Mitzvah of taking Alice in, once again we have been blessed. Alice was a quiet, unassuming individual who was very pleasant to have around. Since I retired, her rent money helped a bit even though it is much lower than the going rate, since she was an elderly woman. Alice was also very good with children. My grandchildren loved her. She saved the day when she was a back-up for Michelle who was baby-sitting for Benjamin and developed a severe headache. Alice also was very helpful in the kitchen washing dishes, and helped me to cut vegetables when I broke my arm. She had a sharp mind and fitted in with the family. She played a good game of scrabble until the age of 91 until her sight was failing! She would rake leaves like a 30-year old; there was no stopping her! Most of all we can benefit from the wisdom of her years. I had a sample of that when Alice became a peacemaker. Felicia and I were planning the Thanksgiving menu. We became involved in an argument about what to eliminate since there were too many items to cook. As usual, I was planning more than I could handle, but at the moment, I refused to see that. Alice came in and said, "This is not a restaurant! Why do you have to offer everyone three choices of soup, turkey, meat, etc."? You serve one thing of each and if anyone doesn't like it, they can go home! (I recently read a phrase posted on someone's refrigerator; "There are two choices for dinner; like it or leave it") If you don't do that, you will wear yourself out and aggravate your back problem. What kind of Thanksgiving will that be?" I listened to her and realized as I was cooking that she was absolutely right!

Although Alice came for a temporary short stay, Max told her that he considered her as part of the family and she could stay as long as she wants.

Once in a while, Alice would comment on the problems with her mother's house upstate. It required much repair work and it was difficult for her to get upstate and supervise any of the work. She received notices from the town that if no repairs were made, the house would have to be torn down. It was becoming a hazard. If the home were demolished, she would be responsible for demolition fees. Alice felt helpless and worried about the house.

One afternoon, I took Alice with me to visit my daughter and children in Greenlawn. When I returned home with Alice, there was a man and a woman sitting in my living room. They were talking to Max. I assumed they were our new neighbors that just bought the house next door to us. I guessed wrong! They were looking for Alice! They lived in the town of Hurley where Alice's mother's house was. They owned a vegetable farm and ran a roadside stand in Hurley. They knew of the impending demolition of the house and were interested in buying it from Alice! Tracking down where Alice lived was no easy feat for them because she used only a post office box for her address. They followed several leads and were finally told to try the Senior Citizen's group she attended. Many people in town would notice Alice for she was known for walking great distances in all kinds of weather. Even the postman knew her and when questioned by the man and woman, he directed them to our house. It seems these people want to restore the home since it is a historical site. It is an 11-room wood frame house built in 1810! They also want to restore the furniture and make the house available to tourists. Alice mentioned that her mother always lamented that her possessions would be thrown out. The restoration would solve that problem also. It seems that God answered her prayers! She sold the house to them. God works in strange ways!

Alice lived with us five years and suffered another stroke. Alice passed away recently. God rest her soul.

Chapter 9:

ON CATS AND DOGS

A DOG AT THE CEMETARY

Approximately one year after my mother's death, I had an unveiling for the headstone of her grave, which is a traditional Jewish custom. Friends and family attended. I returned to the gravesite a week later to be alone at my mother's grave. Only Max accompanied me. I became very emotional. I was in tears and was actually kneeling at her grave, which I don't believe is permissible for a Jewish person to do. Max tried hard to console me before I got carried away. Suddenly, a black dog appeared from virtually nowhere and came over to me and licked the tears off my face. "He must be a stray," I observed, as I kept petting him. "We should go to the cemetery office to see what to do with him." suggested Max. No one had reported a missing dog and we decided to take him home with us till we found a home for him. As I was riding home with him in my lap, I realized that he had come seemingly out of nowhere and had intervened at the right time for my attention was now focused on getting him a home. Once home, he proved to be a handful. He was very energetic...(a retriever). He jumped over everything and tore the place apart. Handling four children, one of which was an infant, and having a big Lassie-type collie, which did not get along with him spelled "stress". I did not need this! But we could not find a home for him. No one seemed to want a dog! One day, we went out for a short time, and decided to lock him in the bathroom so he could not destroy the rest of the house. When we arrived home, we found the plastic shower curtains chewed all the way up. I was at my wit's end. I simply prayed. No longer had I finished praying when the deliveryman for my groceries came to the door. He petted the dog and seemed to like him. "You wouldn't want to keep this dog, would you?" I anxiously asked. He looked him over and decided that he would make a great companion for his German shepherd dog at home, and proceeded immediately to walk out with the dog!

Max and I feel that this dog was sent to me at the right time to keep me from dwelling on my mother. Also, when he became a great burden, God relieved me of him. In the same vein, when my mother's illness became incurable, and she had great suffering, God relieved her of her burdens. It took this mysterious find of a dog to open my eyes to this and I was able to let go of obsessing about the loss of my mother.

MONIQUE

It all began when Butch, our faithful old dog of 14 years passed away. Butch had arthritis and we kept him up to the point where it was impossible to care for him. We felt that he was not getting much joy out of his life due to pain and immobility. Sadly, we finally had to put him to sleep. Time passed and it was hard to replace him psychologically. Michelle, who was 16 at the time, finally awakened us to our responsibility toward her with: "Okay, so what are we doing? Are we getting a dog or an alarm system like you promised? I don't feel safe at home when I'm alone." She was right; we had been procrastinating, partly from loyalty to Butch's memory and also the thought of taking on another dog seemed like a big undertaking, but we had to do something. Max preferred having a dog to an alarm system and I agreed with him. Before we knew it, the next day, we decided to "just take a look" at the nearest animal shelter. How can you "just take a look" when you see these animals begging to be released from their caged environment and you know you have the opportunity to give one of them a good home. We took several dogs out of their kennel to see how they would react to us, but none of them seemed to respond. There was one very beautiful dog that I had apprehensions about. It was a Border collie that paced her cage more than the others. Probably a very restless, "hyper" dog I thought. But we took her out of the cage anyway and to our surprise found that she was the only dog that was able to focus her eyes on us, (actually looked you straight in the face) and showed much affection when petted. Ironically, she had the same exact colors as Butch, a shiny coat of black hair with white markings on her chest and paws. It was "love at first sight" for Michelle. She opted to take "Monique" home and that we did! What a strange name for a dog, I thought but later when Monique was home with us, I could guess why the former owners had named her thus. She would sit straight up at attention when she wanted to be petted, pointing her nose and turning her head sideways showing her beautiful profile, extending her paw, as if she were modeling. What a lady! The name "Monique" seemed to fit her perfectly.

When people saw our new dog, they were taken aback at the similarity between her and Butch in coloring. My neighbor walking from afar seeing this black, energetic bundle of fur coming down the street, did not know that Butch had died. He did a double take, trying to figure out how an old arthritic dog could have been "resurrected" to this point of recovery and recognized she was a newcomer as he came closer.

My son Larry had moved back home and Monique became "his" dog. He played with her and "spoiled" her with special food and gave her attention to the point where he was exhausted (not the dog, though!) I was right about the "hyper" part. She had boundless energy.

Monique would guard Larry's bed at night when he slept. If Max or I would pass the room where Larry was sleeping, we were greeted by growls from Monique. So much for acknowledging the hand that feeds you.

However, when Larry was not home in the evening, Monique would transfer her watch-post upstairs to Michelle's room and guard her (and growl at us if we attempted to enter her room. Therefore, Michelle was No. 2. Max and I who fed the dog, walked the dog, responsible for vet bills, etc. were at the bottom of the list in order of her preference.

No gratitude! But she did show much affection and loyalty to all the family. When we were out in the backyard, she stayed close by us, never running onto anyone else's property.

I would often get comments from people when I walked Monique on how beautiful she was. She never soiled the house. Yes, Monique was the perfect dog!

After Monique was with us for about eight months, late one evening, Larry noticed that she had an epileptic seizure. She quickly stood up from it, as if nothing had happened. It happened several times that evening. However, the next morning and throughout the day, she seemed fine. Larry stayed home from work that day due to an upset stomach. He felt better later and went out to get her a new Frisbee. She loved catching Frisbees and received much exercise that day. She feasted on lamb stew meat that day, a cheap cut I had gotten from the butcher. She seemed to enjoy it. All in all, she was enjoying a perfect day with her favorite person spending a lot of time with her. At about 4pm, I took the car out to do some quick shopping for an hour. Upon my return, Michelle greeted me with hysterical sobs. "Monique is dead", she cried. I could NOT believe what I was hearing. But there she was, this young, once energetic dog, lying motionless on the den floor. Larry explained that she had gone into another epileptic fit. Michelle went to work that afternoon as a waitress even though she was very upset. I don't know how she did it. Larry, needless to stay was devastated. He called his brother, Ed from nearby Kings Park and he came to help dig a deep ditch in the back yard. When Max came home from work we buried Monique and said farewell to an "angel" of a dog if there ever was one. Her grave was marked by the new Frisbee, which she loved so much. Earlier that afternoon, a few hours before she died, Larry watched a video. In it, there was a dog that looked exactly like Monique, which is quite unusual. Yes, Monique WAS unique. The dog in the video had the same markings as Monique and moved in the same manner. In the film, a woman dreams that this dog is dead and you see the dog stretched out in the exact same position, as Monique was when she died. Larry showed me this part of the video before he returned it to the store. I stared in disbelief. Was Larry's viewing of this tape earlier in the day a message of the tragic event that was to occur?

Whatever it was, I would like to believe that Monique is soaring on high, catching a Frisbee in the heights of heaven!

A CAT STORY

He sat on my desk in a crate, sleeping away; a small, very thin, curled-up ball of gray fluff. Many parents of the day-care children had been contacted to see if they would adopt this adorable, but pathetic looking critter that had been found on the property of the synagogue where I worked. Since no one seemed to comply, he was placed on my desk because I was known as a "softie".

"Call Max, my co-worker urged. I was hesitant, apprehending what Max's reply would be since there already was a cat in our home that belonged to Michelle, our youngest daughter, who was 20 at the time. Besides, we owned a dog and had two parakeets. After some convincing about how nobody was going to take him, Max relented with "only if he is left to be fed outside!" "Anything you say!" I obliged, and was happy that the cat would be able to get at least that minimum of care.

It was 5 o'clock and I was getting set to go home with this kitten and I mentioned that it would be a good idea to cover the crate so that he would not be able to get out while I was driving. I was assured that he had been sleeping all day, not to worry. As I went to the parking lot with this "treasure", the children from the day- care wanted to take a last glimpse of the kitten and, of course, he woke up. As I put the crate into the car on the back seat, I noticed his eyes closing and assumed he would be all right. No sooner had I entered onto Hempstead

Turnpike, I heard a soft "meow" that seemed to be coming dangerously close to me. Sure enough, what I had suspected was happening. The cat was going toward the break pedal and before I knew it, he had disappeared into the opening under the gas pedal with just his tail protruding. This was rush hour and cars were in back and ahead of me as I waited to make a U-turn. Of course, I could not step on the gas for fear of crushing him. I quickly yanked him out of the opening by his tail and placed him on my lap, holding him with one hand and driving with the other. As soon as the car began moving, he calmed down and stayed on my lap. During the 20-minute ride home, he once tried crawling up on my shoulder but I held him back tightly. As I finally pulled into our driveway, I breathed a sigh of relief and thanked God that we both made it home safely.

Max seemed happy with the kitten and immediately allowed him access to our home. He was introduced to Tabasco, which was Michelle's female cat. Tabasco seemed to "mother" him and when he started running off the property, Tabasco seemed to be "herding" him to stay around the house by running in the opposite direction to distract him. They did have skirmishes once in a while, dog, included. In the evening, "A-1", as we called him (to go with Tabasco sauce) would climb on Michelle's head when she went to sleep and claw her. Nevertheless, when Michelle moved out of the house, she decided to take A-1 with her to keep Tabasco company. Meanwhile, Max being home and retired had become attached to A-1. (He called him "Ketzie") The cat followed him everywhere and he would feed him and put him in for a nap like you would a baby. However, we allowed Michelle to take the cat because we thought the two cats would be good for each other, but we missed him very much. Within a few days, Michelle returned with A-1 in her arms. "You can have this crazy cat! He fights with Tabasco and doesn't leave me alone!" We were so thrilled to have him back! As the weeks went by, he seemed to calm down and went out frequently in the back yard. He grew into a beautiful, large gray and black striped cat with big green eyes and white gloved paws.

A child in the Hebrew School of the synagogue where I worked reported seeing a rat or mouse in the bathroom. During the few years I worked at the Temple, I had never seen any rodent. We did have a squirrel once. An exterminating service came periodically. We thought the child had mistaken a "dust bunny" for a mouse. However, I decided to bring A-1 in to do his "work" anyway, just to make sure. After all, he was originally found on the synagogue property and he was coming back to "pay his dues". I was a little apprehensive about keeping him at work with me. I thought it would be similar to having a three-year old child let loose in my office. At first, he very dutifully inspected all the nooks and crannies in the office. He jumped off the counter which was about four feet high and it was amusing to watch him trying to get back up with just his white paws appearing up over the counter, but he made it! Like climbing a tree, I guess. He ate the food I brought and picked the most comfortable chair in the office and fell asleep in it. After lunch, we decided to send him to "work" and placed him in the bathroom, but he did not find any rat or mouse. The day-care worker who originally found him marveled at how big he had become and the day-care director enjoyed him also, remarking how well behaved he was. He appreciated all the attention and then went to sleep for the rest of the afternoon in the padded chair. As I was finishing up my work for the day, he awoke and decided to sit right in front of me on my desk on top of my work! He would do this to Max at home when he was reading the newspaper; place himself in the middle of the newspaper, which meant "Pay attention to ME, now! I gently picked him up and placed him alongside my work as I continued putting postage stamps on the mail. He grabbed the stamp container and it became a toy for him. I rescued the stamps out of the container and returned the empty container to him. He chased it around the office while I completed my work. (Just like a three-year old!) We then went home. All, in all, it had been a very pleasant day; my office was not wrecked and it was established that there was no rodent in the bathroom.

A-1 had special television programs he liked. He would, of course, watch only animal programs, with cats, lions, tigers, etc. and try to catch them as they moved on the screen. Any other programs bored him and he would go to sleep.

By saving A-1 from being a stray cat, we were blessed. He had become a companion to Max when I was at work and followed him everywhere. At the end of the day when I returned home, I looked forward to holding him and hearing his soft purr of contentment.

About eight months later, after I returned home from work, I witnessed something I had never experienced in all our 37 years of marriage. Max was crying! He did not even shed a tear when his mother and father passed away or for any other situation! I could not distinguish what he was saying. My first thought was that something had happened to him physically since he recently had tests for colon and prostate cancer, which thank God proved negative, but I soon realized he was talking about the cat! Max had gone shopping early in the morning, which was not his usual schedule. He would always go in the afternoon. We had a rule that whenever we left the house, we would take in the cat. Even though he seemed to stay close to home in the backyard when we were home, we did not want to take a chance when we left for we lived next to a main road. That morning, Max could not find A-1 before he left and decided that he would be all right and went shopping for several hours. Upon his return a man approached him and asked him if he owned a gray cat. Max was informed that A-1 had been killed by a car!

There was no doubt that this had been Max's cat. "He gave me his whole soul!" He sobbed as I held him close and tried to comfort him. Max blamed himself for leaving the cat outside while he went shopping but I tried to convince him that it could have happened at any time. Max and I refused to keep a cat in the house all the time because we felt it was not natural to keep them always confined, not being able to be free out in nature, to run and climb trees, etc.

I remembered that a few days before the cat died, A-1 and the dog seemed to have made peace with each other; the cat going up to the dog and nuzzling her which appeared almost like they were kissing. Since the time Michelle brought back A1, calling him a "devil" cat because he had scratched her head and body pretty badly, he became what she then called a "mush" cat. He calmed down with us old folks and became very loving. The night before he was killed, he was laying on my left side (next to my heart) sleeping peacefully with his white-gloved paws crossed over while I watched television.

I have become interested in Kabbalah, which believes in reincarnation, and I gave Max my interpretation of this traumatic event. It seemed to calm him down. In Kabbalah, it is believed that animals have souls and that they are usually "finishing" making up correction from past lives for a short period required (since animals don't usually live as long as humans.) A-1 came to us like a "lion"; he left like a "lamb". He matured and calmed down and made peace with humanity and even with the animal kingdom (the dog). In the Jewish faith, we are allowed to question and ponder, but I do not believe we are allowed to judge God's final decisions for we are mere humans and there is so much we do not know and understand, but must trust the God that created us. Wherever "Ketzie" is, God rest his soul! We love him!

Chapter 10:

TZEDAKAH (DONATIONS)

FEED THE HUNGRY

I like to save store coupons. One Friday afternoon before Shabbat, I was racing around the supermarket in order to complete my errands before sundown, which starts the Jewish Sabbath. I had several coupons, one of which stated that if you spent $30 or more in the store, you would get a $5 deduction on your order. I was in too much of a hurry to calculate my order to see if I reached the required amount. When I reached the register, it showed that I had $12 worth of coupons. With that much of a reduction, I doubted that I would make the $30 total. On the counter, I spotted the tear-off coupon for charity to "Feed the Hungry" that I usually take when shopping. One of the reasons I donate to this charity, besides the fact that it is a humane thing to do, is that it is a direct commandment from the Bible to "feed the hungry". As I handed the tear-off donation to the cashier, I had a feeling that this would tide me over to make the $30. It did!

Talk about casting your bread upon the waters coming back to you; this time it didn't even have time to swim out before its return!

PASSOVER TZEDAKAH

It was before the Holiday of Passover and my son Ed was making an inventory of the Chametz (food items that contained leaven) that were in his home. It is customary for Jewish people to sell their Chametz to a non-Jew (usually through a Rabbi as an intermediary) since we are forbidden to eat bread on Passover. The total value of my son Ed's foodstuffs that were Chametz came to $28. At the time of the sale, a donation is usually made to a charity or a synagogue. Ed's wife Lauren suggested that they should contribute to the congregation to help cover the food for kiddush when they go to services on Shabbat. She determined that the amount should be $7 for each aliyah that Ed was given when he went up to the Torah. Since he was given 4 aliyahs that would come to $28! This was the same amount as the total of the Chametz. That evening Ed was watching the lottery numbers on television. He was never in the past able to guess even one number correctly. Just before the last number came up, he thought to himself, "I bet it's 28". It was! "What is so important about the number 28?" he thought. And then it dawned upon him! His wife's birthday is May 28 and his son's is January 28!

A BEGGAR IN TOWN

An acquaintance related this story to me. She was in the midst of reading a book written by a Rabbi's wife in which the author relates stories about giving tzedakah to people on the street. After reading the chapter, she realized that she had never come across a beggar in the town where she lives. Whenever her and her husband gave charity it was through an organization where you don't get to see the recipients personally. That very same day, when she went shopping, a disheveled man approached her for money for a cup of coffee. After she made her contribution to him, she noticed that he did not remain to ask for help from other people. She assumed he went off to get something to eat. Of course, it gave her a good feeling to know that she had helped someone directly. She found it strange that this occurred so soon after reading the chapter on tzedakah, especially since beggars were a very rare occurrence in her area. It's seems as if God planted the beggar in her midst so that she could experience the mitzvah of giving charity personally!

A DONATION TO ISRAEL

There is a Temple member where I worked at the Synagogue that has Multiple Sclerosis. I received a call from her at the office that she was being hospitalized and that she was probably going into rehab. She sounded very depressed. I told her that I would pray for her and added her name to the get-well list at the Temple. That Shabbat I was home with what was probably the flu. I was reading a Kabbalah book and came across a symbol for healing. I thought of her. Here I was feeling physically miserable, but realized that the flu was a temporary situation whereas hers was of a more permanent nature. The chapter I was reading on healing mentioned that if you pray for someone and meditate on the Hebrew letters, the healing would come through for you also. I prayed for her and remembered that she was a "Zionist" like myself. We were once discussing how when leaving Israel on our trip home we would cry our eyes out! When a Mishaberach (prayer for healing) is said in the Temple, it is customary to give a donation to some worthy cause. Knowing that she would be happy if she knew I made a donation to Israel, I did just that. On my next call to her, she informed me that there was a new drug being administered to her that was supposed to help stop the progression of her disease. It came from Israel!

Chapter 11:

ISRAEL

FIRST TRIP

I am sitting on the sands of a beach on the shores of Long Island and, ironically, this is being written on a sheet of stationery from a Tel Aviv hotel (a piece of paper salvaged from my purse as I was looking for something to write on). The letterhead brings back memories. For years I had dreamed of going to Israel but with raising five children and attending to a sick, aging father, I was not able to make my first trip till 1987. Max and I went with Felicia and Michelle, my two youngest children. It was a wonderful trip. I was so enthused by Israel that I wanted to make Aliya (live there). Max, although he enjoyed visiting the country had no desire to live there. Upon our return home, one Sabbath morning, on the way to the Temple, we were discussing the subject. I mentioned that I was sure it was mentioned in the Torah that a Jew should live in Israel. That very morning, during the sermon, our Rabbi stated that the commandment to live in Israel is mentioned in the Torah more than any other. I really believe that it was God trying to tell us something.

There are mystical writings that prophesy that, believe it or not, the safest place to be living in the future for the Jews will be Israel. When I mention this to Max, he disagrees and points to all the problems that Israel has and believes that it would be dangerous to live there. At about the time we had this discussion I came across this verse from the Zohar:

> If a man loves a woman who lives in a
>   street of tanners
>
> If she were not there he would never go
>   into it
>
> But because she is there it seems to him
>   like a
>
> Street of spice makers where all the sweet
>   scents of the world are to be found
>
> So "even when they are in the land of their

enemies" which is the street of tanners,

"I will not abhor or reject them",
>because of that bride in their midst,
>the beloved of my soul who abides
>there.

Of course, I see the "street of tanners" as Israel and the "bride in their midst" is God.

When I was in Jerusalem, I felt a strong yearning to visit the Wall at least once a day, as if something was pulling me toward it. When I returned to the States I mentioned this to a friend and he said he felt the same way when he was there. On one of my visits to the Wall, as I was leaving, about halfway out of the court, I experienced sort of an electrical vibration through my body that is hard to describe. It was a warm feeling of peace, and euphoria. As I moved further away from the Wall, this glow slowly diminished. I believe this area is very special and that I felt the presence of God there. Years later, I saw a program on television involving the mystery of where the Ark of the Covenant was to be found. Some believe it to be under the Temple near the Wall. The Ark was said to be made with gold in such a way that it could give off electrical charges. Perhaps this is what I felt when I was in the Plaza at the Wall!

THE SAND-DIAL

Two years later, upon his graduation from college, I took my younger son, Ed and my oldest daughter, Sue to Israel. While in Haifa, we visited the Rabbi that performed the Bar Mitzvah for my son years ago. I was taken aback when my son announced to him that the next day when we were to visit a diamond factory that he was considering buying an engagement ring for his girl. The next day while in Safed, a village of mystics, we walked down a street where much of their beautiful artwork was sold. I remember on my first trip looking longingly at a piece of art of The Book of Ruth done in small Hebrew lettering shaped in a picture of a women supposed to be the likeness of Ruth. It was too expensive for me to purchase. On the second trip the same type of work was being sold in different portions of the Bible pictured in Hebrew lettering. Prints of the original works were being sold by the artists, which made it more affordable. I chose Ecclesiastes, which was a picture of a sand-dial depicting the sand sifting into the lower half of the glass. The artist explained his work to me: The sand is "time" as Ecclesiastes states, positive and negative aspects of time, i.e. "A time to be born, a time to die, etc. He stated that the sand in the lower half of the glass was the time that has passed with all the negative occurrences and that NOW in the upper half, all the positive good stuff was coming down! That evening, we visited the diamond factory and my son purchased the ring as he said he would! I was on cloud nine! The girl he planned to marry was as ideal a prospective spouse as I could hope for any of my children! Were indeed the sands of time changing for the better as the mystic had prophesied! It certainly seemed so.

As we were visiting the Ramon Crater, I received another message. The guide was explaining how the type of animals that once roamed this area had been replaced to this now barren land as an experiment to see if they could survive. They were released and not seen for several months and then a litter of their young were spotted, evidence of their ability to survive in a land that was once occupied by their ancestors. I see this as a parallel to the story of the Jewish people. We reclaimed the barren land of our forefathers and in its rocks and desert we have struggled to survive. With determination, hard work and God's help and Divine guidance, miracles have been performed in the land. Am Yisroel Chai! (The Nation Israel lives!)

THE RED CARPET

My third trip to Israel was sandwiched in between Michelle's bat mitzvah in the states and Ed's wedding; all within a three-month period (June - Michelle's bat mitzvah in the states; - July - her bat-mitzvah in Israel with Max and myself; August - Ed's wedding!) I was told that we were crazy to undertake so many things so close together. That summer of 1990 proved to be one of the most memorable, exhilarating ones of our lives!

Michelle had a choice of having her bat-mitzvah reception in our home and then going to Israel with Mom and Dad and having a bat-mitzvah again in Israel or having the reception in a fancy hall. I was so happy and proud that she chose Israel over the "big party". When were looking at brochures of Israel, we discovered that we could make the trip this time in all 5-star hotels for the same price we had traveled before with less frills. When we met Limor, an Israeli friend of ours, (a chapter is devoted to her elsewhere in this book) in Tel Aviv, we were walking down Dizengorf St. in search of a wedding gown for her. Limor was planning to get married in October of that year. As we were walking, I mentioned to her how this trip was "like a dream", everything was so perfect and the service we were getting in the hotels was "red carpet" treatment. As soon as I mentioned "red carpet", she motioned me to look down at my feet. There in the middle of the street was a red carpet! We proceeded to walk over it, laughing hysterically in disbelief. The weeks that followed proved to live up to this "red-carpet". It was as if God was saying, "This is the best! Make sure you know it and enjoy!

Our last few days in Israel on that trip, were spent in Hertzelia, which is a beach resort. I remember being served dinner outside on the veranda of the hotel overlooking the Mediterranean Sea. It was twilight and the moon appeared above the water as white-gloved waiters served us a sumptuous meal. It was so beautiful, it seemed unreal. But as we were headed home, the news of a terrorist attack of a patrol boat not too far from Hertzelia shocked us into reality. It was about that time that the Kuwait War began.

Two years later, after Limor was married and had just had a baby, she implored us to come visit. As my job just offered one week of vacation, and the economy was shaky, I could not see how we could do it. Michelle would have liked to join her boyfriend on a Pilgrimage to Israel for six weeks but that was too expensive and she had been on tours twice already. I delayed writing to my friend. I did not know what to tell her. Then one Sabbath, in synagogue during the Amidah prayer, my eye hit the phrase "May it be Thy will, O Lord Our God and God of our fathers, to lead us joyfully back to our land, and to establish us within its borders....." After services, when we returned to our car, Michelle said, "I have to go to Israel! This morning I read in the prayers about 'going back to our land, and being established in its borders".

I found it uncanny that both of us had received the same message at the same time! I had to follow through on this. It seemed destined. That week I spoke to Max about sending only Michelle to Limor to Israel to help with the baby during the summer. To my surprise, he agreed readily. Michelle would be able to see Mike, her boyfriend, there after he completed his Pilgrimage and they would be able to go on the plane together.

LARRY'S TURN

I made sure that each of my children had a taste of Israel. Since we did not have money to go all at once with our big family, we took separate trips. It was finally Larry's turn to go. I went alone with him to save money. One of the memorable experiences that Larry was looking forward to and enjoyed was a kayak trip down the Jordan River. Larry's views about Israeli politics changed radically when he visited and took the tours with a very learned scholar and historian who was our tour guide. Being in the country and listening to the tour guide, he became sympathetic to the problems that Israel has.

ED AT THE TECHNION

Our next trip was when Ed and Lauren lived in Israel in Haifa. Ed was doing a post-doc at the Technion at the time. Haifa is very beautiful. I was impressed with its picturesque hills, beaches, seaport and exotic flowers. Ed took us to see his lab at the Technion. I was proud that Ed was working on a project in conjunction with his Alma Mater, Rensselaer, that would benefit both Israel and the US.

THE BIRTH OF YOSEF

My next trip was to visit Yosef, born to Ed and Lauren. He is my first grandchild and he is a Sabra (a native of Israel)! While I was there, I had a taste of every-day life in Israel. I shopped in the supermarkets and organized a party for Yosef's

Pidyon Ha Ben. This is a Jewish traditional ceremony for the redeeming of the first-born son, which dates back to bible times. Coins are exchanged and prayers are chanted. I was awed by the fact that so many people in the Orthodox Jewish community responded by coming to this ceremony. It is a tight-knit community and they help to share each other's joys and sorrows.

A TRIP OF SUPPORT

This trip was taken to support tourism at a time when it appeared quite dangerous to visit the country.

We had faith that God would watch over us. I received a message from the Bible and prayer book that angels are behind us and before us. We booked hotels in Tel Aviv, Jerusalem, Eilat and the Dead Sea, with a tour to Safed and Haifa and visits to friends in Hod Hasharon, and Raanana.

We visited my friend Limor and her family and took a guide with her and her husband, Avi, to Mt.

Karkom in the Negev Desert. Avi sat in the back seat of the jeep as we rode over a very bumpy, rough path. It was a long trip and he was feeling the bumps the most. He had been an officer in the Israeli army and certainly had his fill of riding through the desert. I could hear him mumbling to himself most of the way about why was he doing this and that he must be crazy and that his friends are mishegoyam (crazy people)! However, after he climbed Mt. Karkom he felt differently. This mountain is believed to be the real Mt. Sinai where Moses received the Ten Commandments. On our return to the US, we saw a program on television with the Italian archaeologist that discovered twelve stones and what appeared to be an alter at the base of this mountain. This fits in with the Torah portion in which Moses built an alter and set up twelve pillars symbolizing the twelve tribes of Israel. At the top of the mountain were inscriptions that resembled a tablet with ten sections. When we were there, our guide pointed out all of this to us. There were other factors that seemed to lend credence to this being the right mountain. There were pieces of flint found which was used at the time and certain shrubbery at the base of the mountain, which could support cattle. The guide also showed me a plant growing there whose leaves could sustain humans. However, the time did not seem to coincide with that in the Bible.

We also visited Safed, which is one of my favorite places in Israel. It is a city known for Jewish mysticism, a center for Kabbalists through the ages. There is an artist's colony there whose artists paint spiritual pictures, many of which use the Hebrew letters from the bible stories to form beautiful paintings. On every trip, I try to purchase copies of them. On this trip, our tour guide who is a friend of ours directed us to one of the artist shops. The artist appeared and directed me to a poster painting that he created of an 18-point star in blue and white with a "chai" symbol in the center. The number 18 (chai in Hebrew) represents life. It was so beautiful! It was ironic, since 18 is "my" number. I was born on the 18th against the odds, for my mother had a heart condition which her doctor thought would be life-threatening for her to carry through the pregnancy. However, we both survived, and here once again, by the Grace of God, I survived this "risky" trip and was able to take home this beautiful, symbolic painting of life! The "chai" poster had even more significance to me when I returned home to the States. I was pleasantly surprised to learn that the couple that I had put a prayer in the wall for fertility was pregnant! They confirmed that the time we were at the Wall coincided with the time of conception!

Our tour guide also showed us an old canon called a Davidka. At the start of the 1948 War of Independence, Safed's Jewish population consisted of mostly elderly, religious people totaling less than 2,000. They were forced to defend themselves against an Arab attack of 6,000.

Being a religious group, the Jews were not armed. They resorted to using an old canon (Davidka) which could not cause much physical harm, but were able to cause it to make such a loud noise that it scared the Arabs. Immediately following the use of the canon, a thunderstorm occurred which is unknown to occur at that time of year. This added to the fright of the Arabs. They fled from the city! This is known as the "Miracle of Safed"!

The tour guide took us into one of the ancient synagogues in Safed and since he was also a rabbi, he gave us a short sermon. I cannot remember the details of the sermon, but I do remember coming out of the synagogue on a spiritual high, feeling at one with God and the universe!

Chapter 12:

THE SABBATH

THE GARAGE DOOR

Before I moved to Long Island, our family lived in Rego Park. We are a Conservative Jewish family, but I would walk (sometimes run if we were late) to synagogue on the Sabbath with my children since the Temple was not too far away. At the time, Max was not as observant as I was in keeping Sabbath and attending synagogue. He felt that since we could not travel on Sabbath and visit friends and family that he did not have enough of the weekend to do work around the house. When he worked on the Sabbath, it caused many arguments between us. One sunny Sabbath afternoon, I remember sitting under the large maple tree in our backyard reading a book. Much to my disappointment, Max was working on the garage door and the sound of the saw just grated on my nerves. Suddenly, the heavy door came crashing down and missed him by a hair's breath! It shook him up and when I said "God is warning you to rest!" he did not argue with me. He did not work on Sabbath after this incident. We soon moved to Long Island and bought a house that was three miles from any Conservative synagogue. I agreed to ride to synagogue on Sabbath and in return, he promised he would attend synagogue more often. In the former temple in Rego Park, the people saw Max so seldom that they thought I was a widow (God forbid) with 4 children. His attendance changed radically when we were on Long Island. He became so involved that he took the position of Ritual Chairman in the Temple!

The garage door falling years ago was a blessing. We both now enjoy a restful Sabbath and Max looks forward to the peace that results from its observance.

A DEADLINE IN BIO

It was a late Friday afternoon in May. My daughter Felicia was struggling to finish her presentation for her bio class, which was due the next morning. The sun had begun to set, ushering in the

Sabbath. All that was left to do on the thesis was reproduce the transparencies she would be using to demonstrate. The machine, however, refused to respond. The work was "melting" causing the print to disappear. Over and over again she tried, but to no avail. Several hours later, her fiancé, Keith, came by and he tried it and was successful. As Felicia sees it "Being that I try to observe the Sabbath as much as possible, it seems as if God was trying to keep me from breaking the Sabbath by keeping me from reproducing the copies". A Rabbi once said the more observant you are, the greater the responsibility!

THE SUBMERSIBLE

This episode occurred when Ed was doing an engineering post-doc at Johns Hopkins. Actually, a part of the work involved marine biology. For one of his experiments, he was to go down in a submersible off the coast of Gloucester, Massachusetts to search for "micro-lobsters" known as copepods. These tiny creatures give off light when they sense danger. When this happens, it makes the location of a submarine noticeable. Ed was to go down approximately 700 feet to search the waters and image copepods with a laser. This can be a dangerous mission. Two men have died years ago in a previous experiment when there was a malfunction in the equipment.

From the outset, even before the crew boarded the ship, Ed had problems in his lab in preparation. He stayed up all night for many nights at the onset of his trip trying to get the laser to produce enough power. Once aboard ship, leaks were spotted in the submersible. This delayed the experiment for several days and involved hard work. Again Ed went without sleep for several nights at a time. This seemed like a trip from hell, both physically and emotionally. Ed continuously struggled to troubleshoot a leaky housing on top of the submersible. As he did this, the submersible kept moving with the rocking of the ship. Not an easy task, by far. Just before Sabbath, they ran into another major problem. The laser was flooded with oil. This was bad news. If even one speck of oil got on any of the 7 mirrors and lenses, the whole experiment would have to be canceled. Ed noticed the oil was on the outside of the mirror, which was not harmful. But they did not know the condition on the inside unless they dismantled the laser. This was never done before on the ship. The rocking of the boat while at sea could cause problems while they were lowering the laser to the deck. Time was of the essence. However, Ed is a Sabbath observer. Everyone depended on him, and even though there was great pressure on him, he refused to work on Sabbath since it is a God-given commandment to rest on this holy day. He informed them that he would continue working immediately after Sabbath and he went to sleep for most of the Sabbath. Needless to say, he was exhausted. Instead of dismantling the laser at sea, they went back to port, since Ed refused to work. When the stars appeared in the sky after Shabbat, Ed resumed working straight through the night.

He discovered that the oil leaks were only on the outside. Had they taken everything apart at sea during Shabbat, the rocking of the boat would have caused the oil to spread INSIDE the laser, which would have been catastrophic. As Ed continued to work after Sabbath, everything started to fall into place. It was decided to go down even though there were slight leaks. On July 4, Independence Day, Ed was underwater and said he felt like he was seeing fireworks; the micro-lobsters lit up the sea and jellyfish were exploding with luminescent confetti. He said it was a sight to behold. The experiment was, after all, a success. Everything worked and they got great pictures. Thank God Ed was safe, for this had been a dangerous undertaking. I am sure God was watching over him!

A WALK ON THE SABBATH DAY

Down the road from my house is an expanse of beautiful landscape that at one time belonged to a horse-race magnate. It now sits in a setting of picturesque homes on rolling hills accompanied by tall pines and other large trees. Feeling depressed after I lost a baby in the sixth month, I decided to take a walk down this beautiful path and was inspired to write this poem:

A POEM OF HOPE

The clouded sky reflected my mood

But on Sabbath, you are not allowed to brood

I noticed the clouds shone

With a radiance of their own

Soft puffs of silver and gray

Filled the heavens in bright array

Above a border of dark green spruce

All nature seemed to know its use

By proclaiming the beauty of their Creator;

God, the most perfect painter

For who can excel His works of art

Their beauty speaks right to the heart

His splendid canvas seemed to say

With all these great works on display

How could there remain a doubt

That the one who brought this all about

Would in His great wisdom be our guide

If we would but in Him confide

And put our trust in Him to care

How much better we would fare

And come to realize in His will

There is a purpose to fulfill

When clouds appear to fill the sky

Sad times in life; we wonder "why?"

Why the suffering and the loss?

All those difficult paths to cross

At these times we may not see

The reason for these clouds to be

But look up and you will find

Beauty in them and sun behind

For the rain they bring will in time grow seed

Bringing to trees the water they need

Though it is beautiful and sad to see

Bright leaves falling from a tree

They bring a promise of what is to be;

The following spring, if we but wait

Wait upon the Lord, for He is great!

THE CLOSING OF THE SABBATH

Shabbat was coming sadly to a close. I had just finished reading a very interesting Kabbalah book. The last chapter was about the three elements of a burning candle; the wick, the blue light and the white light; the wick representing the unifying force of the blue and white light; the blue flame symbolizing the connection with the physical body and the Desire to Receive (drawing up energy from below) which denies spirituality, seeking materialism. The white light rises above both, closest to God and is pure. By fulfilling the mitzvot of the Torah we rise above, similar to the white light, and come closer to God.

I find it very significant that as I finished reading this book with this chapter on the candle, it was time to light the Havdalah candle, which marks the close of the Sabbath. I gazed into the light of the burning Havdalah candle and prayed that I would be able to attain the purity of the white light by fulfilling the mitzvahs of the Torah.

Chapter 13:

ON EMPLOYMENT

I have noticed through the years that jobs fell into my lap at the proper time and when they did not there was a reason for it; mostly because I was not listening to what I believe were Divine messages. I attribute my good fortune to receiving employment at the right time also to the care of the good Lord.

RETURNING TO WORK

After raising five children, the youngest being 10 years at the time, I decided to go back to work. After only working two weeks for the local school district, I realized I was not ready for the high-pressure world out there. With some brush-up on typing and shorthand I decided to give it another try several months later. I saw a job advertised locally for an engineering firm. However, it was full time and I wasn't sure if I was ready for that yet, since I still had two children at home. However, I had made up my mind to call for an interview the next morning.

That morning the phone rang. It was the secretary of the synagogue I belonged to. She wanted to know if I would be interested in taking her place. It was part-time and she thought that with my religious background I would be able to fill the spot. What timing! I know that God had something to do with that. I knew that this job would carry a lot of responsibility, as it was a one-girl office. But I rationalized that "God would help me and I would be in my 'second home', the Synagogue".

I worked at the Temple for two and one-half years and it was very fulfilling to know that I was helping my Synagogue. However, being a member I became quite involved in the political problems of the Temple. After a while, I found it difficult to continue working there and still be able to keep a neutral attitude.

My next job was at a local insurance agency. I was not using my shorthand skills, but as jobs were hard to get I resolved to stick it out. However, when my salary was not adjusted as promised at the proper time, I patiently waited, but to no avail. The reasons given, I felt were not justified. I produced the work in an efficient manner way past the requirements. It was very difficult to get an appointment to speak with the supervisor. I was quite annoyed and vowed to myself that on Monday morning I was just going into the outer office and get things cleared up, one way or another. That Friday afternoon, I went home feeling very upset about my job. I was preparing for the Sabbath when the phone rang. It was a member from the synagogue that I had previously worked for. He was a physical therapist and wanted to know if I was working. "I am, but I feel like throwing in the towel", I grumbled. "How about being my secretary?" he asked. "My secretary is leaving for another job", he said. Here again, the timing was uncanny. At first, I was hesitant, unsure of myself. This job would entail duties I had never tackled before, but then I felt that if God could "drop this job into my lap" at the proper moment again, I certainly must believe that He will help me to carry it through. I accepted the job and worked for him several years, which also proved to be very fulfilling.

As time went on, the practice declined causing him to move his office to his home. He no longer had a need for a full-time secretary.

I remember sitting in the back yard one Sabbath afternoon with the newspaper next to me. I was tempted to look at the "help wanted" ads. As I reach over for the paper to do this, the chair tipped and I suffered some minor injuries. Was God trying to remind me that even "looking" at business ads is not in keeping with the Sabbath?

I had been unemployed for several months, but I had faith that when the right job would come along, God would lead me to it as He had in the past.

I had a friend that was a devout Christian and she continuously reminded me that you have to have faith. "Maybe God does not want you to be working full-time right now. Maybe he wants you to spend more time writing your book," she said. She also mentioned that I should go back to working in a synagogue. She felt that I "belonged" in the synagogue. At the time, I was not eager, insisting that I needed a full-time job. However, she must have been prophetic, for I eventually did work for two synagogues years later. I must say that going on many interviews, endless phone calls and sending uncountable resumes, after a while can wear a person down. My Kabbalah book mentions "feelings of uncertainty" which sometimes creep into a person, of course, are negative. Faith in God negates these feelings. My unemployment insurance had run out, but I thank God that all our important needs were taken care of. While I was in Temple on Sabbath, my son Larry received a call at my home and took the message. He said it was a call from a doctor's office and that they would call me back at 1p.m. I had applied to many medical offices for work and could hardly figure out which ad was responding. Frankly, I was quite upset at having to face a "business" call on the Sabbath. "Why" I thought is God continually trying me; after all I don't want to do business on Sabbath? I picked up one of my Kabbalah books that I reserve for Sabbath reading. The page opened to a paragraph that hit my eye. It was as if God was immediately responding to my query. It spoke about life's obstacles being continuously in our path to the Tree of Life implying that by overcoming these obstacles, we "earn" our way. A few minutes later, my friend called. During the phone conversation, we were cut off; I received a dial tone. When we were again connected, the sound of someone dialing a phone was heard. No one in either of our homes was making a call. The Doctor never called that day, or was that him trying to reach me? Was that a divine intervention in order to keep this business call from disturbing Sabbath? Whatever it was, I was happy that my Sabbath peace was not interrupted by business.

A CROSSWORD PUZZLE

My son Larry, who was also unemployed at the time, compared his situation to a movie he had seen. In the movie, a man is continuously doing a crossword puzzle every day no matter what happened in his life. When asked why, the man responded that it was a "challenge". Larry commented philosophically about his life that he was stuck on line 39 of his crossword puzzle, referring that he was in a rut with his career. I commented that if he would move to the next line 40 or more and try to figure out what he could, Line 39 might resolve itself and it would all come together. "Move on with your life!" was the message and "do all you possibly can. God will take care of the rest". He seemed to agree.

BASIC SKILLS

I was considerably shaken as I left work one late Friday afternoon. I looked forward to celebrating the Sabbath, especially since I had become employed at a job that I found quite difficult to handle. Sabbath was my salvation, but as I drove home, I found it very hard to fight back tears that had welled up in me since the beginning of my employment about a month before.

I had found it almost impossible to handle the heavy-duty phone system at this job. My employer was quite impatient with my ineptness. On my resume, I had stated the truth about my computer skills; that on the Word Perferct 5.1, I had only basic skills and did not claim work experience on this program. My boss, however, expected me to know much more than I did and his parting words to me prior to that Sabbath Eve were to learn EVERYTHING about the program. I felt overwhelmed, since I knew that I did not have the time. I worked a full day and had classes three nights a week and worked on my old job once a week in the evening. When I spoke to my son, Ed, he suggested that I learn as much as I can on the job and he would help me on weekends. However, I was still disconcerted.

Upon attending synagogue services the next morning, there was a Bar Mitzvah taking place. The Rabbi presented the certificate to the Bar Mitzvah boy as he usually does, with the same offering that he gives to all Bar and Bat Mitzvahs; that of attending classes to further their education in Judaic studies. A phrase of his caught my attention that hit home. "You have the BASIC SKILLS, but IT'S NOT ENOUGH; YOU MUST GO ON FROM THAT TO INCREASE YOUR KNOWLEDGE." "Basic skills" were the exact words I used in my resume! And here was a message straight from the pulpit for me to continue to learn.

I went home and that evening, I worked with Ed on the computer. At work, I had an opportunity to use some of the computer functions that I had studied with Ed. My boss was somewhat impressed. Within a few weeks, I had learned a sufficient amount of computer commands to keep my boss happy. However, the heavy phone work still continued to be a problem, and no matter how hard I tried, it just wasn't working out. Wherever, I had worked previously, I always felt that I was an asset to the office. I did not want to continue working at a job in which I was not functioning to capacity and I informed my boss that I would stay on until he was able to replace me with someone else. He said he liked me and that the office was running smoothly because of me, but the phones *were* a big problem. However, he said that at this point I knew enough of the Word Perfect 5.1. Program to work in any office that had it.

So you see, I believe the message I received in synagogue helped me in my everyday business life. Baruch Hashem!

A JOB AND A BROKEN LEG

After I gave notice to the Real Estate office that I would be leaving, I went to work for an engineer. This job involved using the Word Perfect 5.1

program. It did not have heavy phones, but it was also stressful. After working there for over a year, I was beginning to wonder if I could keep on like this. I believe God interceded before the stress did serious damage to me.

It was about this time, one winter evening; I was going to work on my second job for the physical therapist. When he had previously downsized my job several years ago, I maintained working for him about one night a week. This particular night, I parked my newly purchased two-year old car in his driveway and proceeded to walk down the shoveled path. (It had previously snowed). He came out on the porch to see my "new" car and just before I was about to ascend the steps, I found myself on the icy ground in an instant writhing in pain. The pain was too severe for me to move and an ambulance was called. In the Emergency Room, I could see that my leg was quite disfigured. I had compound fractures that required extensive surgery with a metal plate and bone grafts. With

God's help and a good surgeon, I pulled through and was told that I would not be able to drive a car for about three months.

When I returned home, my dear friend, Judy, suggested to me that my work schedule had been too hectic and that in the future, I should work in a Jewish organization where I could get off more time to prepare for Sabbath and that it should be a part-time job. (Meanwhile, my dear friend runs herself ragged with a hectic schedule also. Birds of a feather stick together!) Her words preyed on my mind and I repeated them to my friend Eleanor, who is the wife of a Rabbi I used to work for. She informed me that there was an opening in her Synagogue for a secretary, but that they needed someone immediately. "Sorry, but that's not possible. I cannot drive for another three months", I replied regrettably. It's strange that if this job were offered to me several years ago, I would have deliberated that it was not enough hours, the salary was too low, no insurance, etc. However, it appealed so much to me now!

A few days later, I received a phone call from that synagogue. The Board was going to hire a temporary worker and they would wait until I was healed! If this wasn't from Heaven, I don't know what was! I think back to a few years ago, when my friend was trying to give me the message to slow down with a part-time job and write my book. Since that time, I have had two full-time jobs that were hectic. It had to come to this to realize I have to slow down and do what I have to do!

LAST MINUTE

I remember an instance, where a Rabbi friend of ours was released from his contract. As moving time drew closer, his family became frantic as there was no prospect in sight. He reminded them how several times before, a similar situation presented itself and something always came through at the last minute. He was quite calm and assured them that something would again turn up at the last minute. There were but several days left before the High Holidays, when he received a call from upstate for an interview where he became their Rabbi.

Chapter 14:

ON MONEY

MONEY RETURNED

The person involved in this story did not seem it necessary to write it, perhaps because of her humility. Therefore, I am not using her name.

During work, her employer mistakenly gave her quite a large sum of money. At this time, her personal funds were exhausted and she certainly could have used the extra cash. However, she returned it, much to the surprise of her employer. He said that during the many years in the past, there have been errors, but no one had come forward to return the money. "Well, I guess my momma has taught me right. She taught me that the Torah (Bible) considers it stealing if you do not try to return a lost article to the rightful owner."

Shortly after this episode, she was unexpectedly blessed with extra money that she earned!

MONEY IN THE STREETS

My son Larry, in spite of being a cynic when it comes to "spooky coincidences", (his own words) had to relate this one: "I was on a payphone in Manhattan talking long distance with my girlfriend Joyce (who is now my wife) in L.A. She was telling me how she's a worrier, always was a worrier, but an ex-boyfriend of hers was the opposite. (Why I stayed on the phone (long distance) to hear about an ex-boyfriend, I don't know) But anyway, at that time they didn't even have enough money to buy food. "Don't worry, something will turn up", he tells her. Then they go for a walk and what do you know; he finds $90 in the street. "That's some story". I say, but I'm wondering why she would break up with a prophet to go out with me who was also in a similar financial situation. I was about to pose this interesting question to her when something changed my mind.

"Joyce", I said, "could you hold on?"

"What? What's the matter? Talk!"

"...Baby, I just picked up $60 lying in the street".

"Very funny"!

"Why he got $90 and I got $60 I'll never understand...."

I can't answer that question for Larry but I believe that when a person has exhausted all his efforts in a problem situation, a little faith can go a long way!

'IT'S GOING TO WORK OUT!'

I have a friend who is not financially well off. She relates to me that whenever times were tough, she would tell her children, in a very confident voice, "It's going to work out, you will see! It always did. It was but a few days before her daughter's wedding and money was tight. In fact there wasn't even enough money to pick up her daughter's wedding gown. "Don't worry" Miriam assured her daughter. "You will have your gown." Her daughter was skeptical. Sure enough, a workers' compensation check arrived in the mail that was several months overdue. When her daughter arrived home, she sarcastically asked, "So where is the wedding gown you promised?" "Behind the door" her mother answered. Lynn stood staring at the gown in amazement.

Another time money was sorely needed. Miriam was passing by a bank when she noticed two twenty-dollar bills clipped to a deposit slip that was not filled out. The owner could not, therefore, be established. This was the exact amount that she needed to tide her over. Once, her and her two daughters were about to be dispossessed from their apartment and had nowhere to go. "It will work out", Miriam said. "Wait and see". Within a few hours there was a knock at the door. A neighbor from around the corner had an apartment for them...."God is good!" you will often hear Miriam saying. "Amen" to that!

Think about the times in life when you have urgent problems, but you do not lose hope. I believe it helps to have faith that God will be your help through it all. I've heard it said that God did not split the waters for the Israelites until they had the faith to go in up to their neck. Another example of faith in the Bible is when God tells Abraham that he will be the father of a multitude of nations. Even though he was quite old and childless, on blind faith, he believed Him.

Chapter 15:

B'SHERT

B'shert in Yiddish means "destined to be". I believe not only marriages "made in heaven" are b'shert, but there are also the little everyday episodes that have a meaning and a purpose. For instance, there was:

A BROKEN ARM

I couldn't believe it! Not again! Just 2 years ago, I had broken my wrist quite severely. However, it had healed nicely, Baruch Hashem. Here I was again, sitting on the concrete in pain in the parking lot of the synagogue where I worked. It was Friday afternoon (Erev Shabbat). I had just left the office with some letters to mail for the Temple and was homeward bound. My foot slipped on the broken pavement on the way to my car and I fell. My purse and the letters scattered to the ground. As I looked down at my arm I could see that it had swollen immensely.

Usually on a Friday afternoon, I would close the office and I was the last one out. However, this

Friday, Bar Mitzvah pictures were being taken which does not usually take place on a Friday. Because of this, the Rabbi was in the Synagogue. "Rabbi, Rabbi!" I screamed not knowing if he could hear me through the high wall. I was probably too far from the road for a passer-by to hear me. Baruch Hashem, he came running out to me and called for an ambulance. I was taken to a nearby hospital where surgery was done on the compound fracture.

I do not profess to know why these things kept happening to me. I am not God. Only He knows! But as my friend Hanna said, "Pull out of this bad experience all the good ", and there is good. For instance, I was enjoying the beautiful fall weather. I ordinarily would have been at work. I also lost weight and became more independent realizing all I could do with my left arm. (I am right-handed.) With my left hand, I was able to make challah, cake, stuffed cabbage, chicken soup, etc. Even though I was not able to hold my grandson,

Benjamin, with both arms, I had more time to spend with him. (He lived in our house with his family at the time).

Through this experience, I have once again been made aware of the miraculous healing powers of God and man working together. I was very grateful as I saw the progress in my recuperation. Baruch Hashem!

Another important plus is that I had more time to write this book. Actually, at Yom Kippur services, I came across a passage about praising God daily. Besides my regular daily prayers, I realized that through writing this book, I am continually praising God and so I vowed to make a strong effort to write in "Messages" on a daily basis. I remember reading somewhere in kabbalah literature that if something keeps happening to you repeatedly, there is something that you are failing to do in your life. It is ironic that each time I break a bone, I find that I have more time to write my book. However, this time when I broke my arm, Max indicated that he would like me to retire; that there was too much stress on me. I did retire a few months later and, of course, had more time to dedicate to writing this book. Breaking my arm might have been a strong message to stop and attend to priorities!

THE TABLECLOTH

Ed and Lauren presented us with a beautiful white tablecloth that they purchased from Israel on their return to the US. I had always wanted a special one for Shabbat and holidays and this had Jewish stars and candlesticks embossed on it. The fact that it came from Israel also made it very special. It's beauty brought tears to my eyes as I spread it on the table before the Passover Seder. Later when I told Ed how much I appreciated it, he related to me that when they purchased it in the Israeli store, there were only two left. One would exactly fit our table and the other was a smaller one that exactly fit his mother-in-law's table. B'shert!

A BROKEN FURNACE

There was the time when the heating system in my daughter Felicia's home was not functioning. She piled the newborn baby, Ilan, and her 2-1/2 yr. old son into the car and came to stay with us. My son-in law Keith came after work in the evening. They remained with us for a few days until the broken part in the system was replaced. During that time, Ilan cried quite often. He probably was in pain due to gas. He did not burp easily and I suggested putting him on his stomach. Felicia insisted, as she did at other times, that pediatricians in the past several years advocate infants sleeping on their back. She said "statistics show that there are less crib deaths, since babies have less chance of suffocation with their face up." "I raised five kids on their stomachs, and I think there is more chance of a baby choking on spit-up if they are lying on their back!" I replied. Since Ilan was crying so much, I placed him on my bed on his stomach and volunteered to keep watch over him.

He fell asleep almost immediately and slept 6 hours! The following evenings, Felicia placed him on his stomach in the bassinet and he slept through the nights! Recently I spoke to my niece who works in a day-care facility and she informed me that social services wants the infants sleeping on their stomachs. She said this "old-fashioned" method is returning. When the part was fixed and heat returned to her home, Felicia summed up the above with: "Even though it was a hassle not having heat in my house, it was "b'shert" to come to your house so that I would put Ilan on his stomach and we all could have some peace!

Chapter 16:

CATCHING THE MOMENT

MOTHER'S DAY

A vase stands filled with the beauty of God's work; pink and purple tulips, a few with pointed petals, a rare variety, amidst a background of white dogwood blossoms that appear much larger than they do when on the tree.

Here again is an example of man working with God. Felicia planted those tulips. God provided the seed. I understand the great trauma it must have been for her to cut those flowers for me for Mother's Day for I understand her sensitive soul; her love for God's handiwork and her great desire to allow life to flourish. You did not cut those flowers in vain, Felicia. Besides my being able to see their surface beauty right before me, today they have served another purpose. Standing before me, they reminded me to absorb their beauty and "catch the moment" instead of being absorbed in my problems for who does not have any? Your wise instructions along with this precious mother's day gift was that I was not to ignore these flowers and take them to my room or wherever I was going to be in the house. In so doing, they reminded me of the beauty in the world, and in your soul, Felicia, and not to allow the negative aspects of life to screen out the "purple and pink pointed tulips amidst the dogwood!"

This poem was written as I gazed through my bedroom window at the glorious sight and almost missed the "show" by turning away for a brief period).

SNOW

A heavenly scene on earth; God paints His canvas
    with a white brush.
Behold this beautiful sight ere it turns to slush
Such are our moments on earth to be caught and
    cherished before they disappear
As the melting snow that hours before was so
    white and clear
Adorning each tree as a bride at the scene of a
    wedding.

Which precedes the springtime setting

Of the former brides giving birth to budding
flowers and fruit

For each canvas He paints of the seasons there is
a pattern to suit,

A purpose, as the snow nourishes the ground for
the following season

And perhaps there is another reason

For the canvas changing four times a year

God likes variety too, it seems clear

So let's enjoy it with Him!

Chapter 17:

THIS 'N THAT

A TELEPATHIC CALL

When we lived in Queens and our parents still lived in the Bronx, we would faithfully call them each night to see how they were doing. I remember one evening we could not reach Max's mother Gussie. The phone kept ringing. There was no answer. Several hours passed and I could see the anxious look in Max's eyes. I wished I could relieve him of his anxiety. I had a sudden urge to contact her "through the mind" since we could not reach her by phone. I had a strong suspicion that she was sleeping. Max was standing in the kitchen in front of me and I motioned him to get out of my way. Somehow I felt that if he were in front of me, he would block my "connection" to her. I prayed that she would call and as I did, I KNEW that the phone would ring momentarily. It did! "Hello, how are you?" she asked. "I am sorry for not calling sooner, but I fell asleep for a long time."

PRAYERS AT THE WALL

It is believed that prayers said at the Wall in Jerusalem have more impact; that they go straight up to heaven. People write their wishes on little scraps of paper and place them between the stones in the Wall. There is a couple that I know that was having difficulty conceiving. On one of my trips to Israel, I prayed for them at the Wall. Soon after my visit, I was happy to learn that they would be expecting a baby. A while after this child was born, the same problem arose concerning conception. I was again planning a trip to Israel and for the second time put my prayer in the Wall for them. On my return home, they questioned me about which days I visited the Wall. I was informed that the time coincided with the time of conception of their expected child!

AN UMBILICAL CORD

When Max and I first got married, we lived in an apartment in Rego Park, Queens. After I gave birth to our first child, Susan, I became acquainted with the tenant whose apartment was above mine. We first met, sitting on the benches in the yard, while Sue was sitting in her carriage. The conversation came around to babies and children and "Roz" as she was called confided that she had had several miscarriages. I could relate to her anguish as I had had a miscarriage before I became pregnant with Sue. In the months that followed, Roz became pregnant again. Everything seemed to be going fine this time. Before New Year's Eve of that year, Roz called me up to her apartment. She was quite nervous. Her water had broken and she was in her ninth month. She was taken to a nearby hospital and as she left I wished her well and prayed for her and her baby. Before I went to sleep that night, I wished I knew what was happening to her. We had become very close friends.

About 4AM, I was awakened by a dream I had about an umbilical cord and a baby. At first I was upset, but then I had a good feeling. Roz must have had her baby, I thought and went happily back to sleep. The next morning, Morty, her husband called to tell us that Roz had given birth to a healthy baby girl. However, during labor, the cord was wrapped around the baby's neck and an emergency Caesarian Section was performed.

God had answered our prayers and I guess my strong desire to know what was happening resulted in an ESP dream! Marcy was born New Year's eve, giving her father who was in the accounting field, a nice tax deduction!

CANDLE LIGHTING

It was a late Friday afternoon. I was recuperating in bed after I broke my leg. My son Larry, being the only one home at the time could light the Sabbath candles. While he was doing a last-minute errand for me before Shabbat, I realized I would have to write the prayer out for him for candle lighting. I was looking for something to write with when my "Jerusalem" pen FELL out of my bag as if it knew its mission. Lauren, my daughter-in law from Israel, had given this pen to me. It was a beautiful magenta pen with "Jerusalem" printed in yellow on it with rows of sparkling diamond-like shapes on it. Writing lying down always caused pens to stop writing in mid-stream. However, I was able to complete writing the whole prayer in very clear dark blue ink with this pen without a problem. When I tried it another day for something else I ran into the same problem I usually had. It stopped in the middle.

Special pen for special purposes? By being raised to the Heavens to praise the Lord's name, how could it not work?

MESSAGE FROM A BOOK

I had been upset over an incident I had with a friend. I usually don't like to harbor bad feelings, but found it hard to shake my annoyance with this person. I awoke with this negative feeling and began to pray to God to help me overcome this. Across from my bed hung a poster I had recently purchased on my last trip to Israel when I visited the mystical city of Safed. It was a beautiful picture of a white 18-point star with outgoing deepening shades of blue radiating from it. In Judaism, 18 signifies life. I can relate to that for I was born on the 18th of January due to the bravery of my mother. As I prayed, I gazed at the poster and a good feeling overcame me. My eyes then roamed to the headboard over my bed and fell upon a spiritual book that my daughter Felicia had given to me as a gift. I instinctively knew that there was a message in this book to help me and that whatever page I turned to, the answer would be there. Surely enough, I opened the book to a chapter about people who help you through life by supporting you. It also spoke about the opposite condition; negative people who do not support your dreams, and only see what you lack and not what you have and place limitations on love, growth and life, whose cynicism supports suspicion and unhappiness. The latter described this person to a "T"! The book suggested keeping away from people like this and surrounding yourself with people who have a positive attitude about you and the world and have not limitations on love. After I read this I felt relieved and at peace. I am sure this was a message from God!

THE DOMINO EFFECT

Max and I were picking up our grandson Benjamin from his home to take him to visit his cousins in Stony Brook. His mother had a doctor appointment that day and we would be baby-sitting him. He seemed eager to come with us until Max raised his voice to me when I apparently irritated him about some trivial matter. Immediately Benjamin began crying. He would not allow me to put him in the car seat and was crying for his mother. I finally had to fetch his mother from the house and she informed me that recently he had become very sensitive to any loud voice coming from a male, even his father! From this point the plans for the day were changed completely. Felicia had to take me to the doctor's office with Benjamin so that I could watch him in the car while he slept. When he awoke, he wanted to see his cousin Matthew but it was too late in the day. He was quite upset and I later found out that, of course, his cousin Matthew was disappointed that he did not come. If I had not irritated Max he would not have raised his voice to me and Benjamin would not have become upset. What could have been a nice family visit was canceled. Of course, this was not a major catastrophe, but I thought how peoples' actions could change a whole course of events.

Ironically, that very same evening I was watching a television program that paralleled what had happened that day. However, the consequences were more dramatic. One person was irritable to another and the bad humor spread to many people finally resulting in a possible suicide. A flashback portrayed a much happier scenario for all the people involved had a congenial course been followed. Seeing this the same day reinforced in my mind how important every action of ours is. In Kabbalah (mystical Judaism) it is believed that every single action has an effect throughout the whole universe!

SPILLED MILK

It had been one of those days. My daughter Sue was experiencing a "day out of hell" with her kids. Besides the tantrums from both children, Ava, her one-year old was flinging her food from her high chair. To add to this, her husband Howie and she had been having a little spat. That evening, after the kids were in bed, they both sat down to relax. Howie poured himself a big glass of milk when suddenly the whole glass accidentally spilled on him and onto the floor. After the day Sue had experienced, she was in no mood to be of help in any further mopping up. "Its enough that I have to get spaghetti "off the ceiling" all the time. I can't take this! I'm going for a walk!" she announced, leaving Howie to fend for himself in cleaning up the milk. Later that evening, Sue also poured herself a glass of milk. As she sat down on the couch, she placed the milk on the floor next to her. A book slipped from the couch and knocked over her glass! As she related this episode to me, I could not resist the urge to "analyze" it. "I think God was giving her a gentle reminder to (quoting the Bible) 'be a helpmate' to your spouse!"

LAST HOPE

This was the third synagogue that I had been privileged to work in and hold a secretarial position. It was an early Friday afternoon, near to closing time, to enable employees to go home to prepare for Sabbath.

At approximately that time, a member appeared in search of a prayer book that had accidentally been placed in the racks with other prayer books. It was his son's prayer book that had been especially dedicated to him on his Bar Mitzvah the week before with his name inscribed in the inside cover. This synagogue has a membership of over 300 families and finding this book would be like looking for "a needle in a haystack"! As my fellow employee, George, left for the day, he stated whimsically "It will probably be in the last book you look at!" I decided to help this man in his search of the book. We looked through what seemed like an endless amount of shelves and when we came to the last row of books, he sighed. "I guess it's not here!" I still had a few books to search through and when I came to the last one, I too had almost given up. I noticed a different kind of label in this one, with flourishes on the border of it, thinking it must be an old dedication. I took a double take when the right name appeared in the book. This WAS the one!

When I returned home that evening, there was another search going on. My cousin Hank had lent me a tape about a healer that uses "touch" therapy or Reikki. Since my Russian friend Hanna was visiting me, I thought she might be interested in this tape, as she performs Reikki. It was a very interesting tape, based on a true story. However, it had been misplaced and Hank said that his tapes have no labels on them. We proceeded to look for tapes without labels and we were unsuccessful. This felt like the previous scenario earlier that day and we were about to give up since we had run through many tapes. Then Max happened to pick up a tape on the other side of the entertainment shelves with a label that was marked. "That's it!" I shouted. I had loved the story so much, that I had forgotten that I did mark it, ironically, so that I would not "lose it"!

Two similar situations like this in one day, I felt had a message: When you are searching for something, whether it is for a cure, a job, a spouse, etc., don't give up! For out of the blue, from God, when you least expect it, can come an answer or hope. That is how I met my husband, when I had almost given up, but decided to go on that last blind date! The tape that I found also dealt with a family that was almost about to give up on the life of their daughter but tried one last thing that worked!

MY COUSIN JILL

I believe that while we are living here on earth, the way in which we live leaves messages for the rest of us. If we are doing the right things, it can encourage others to follow. Jill was my first cousin and we became very close when I moved to Long Island in close proximity to her home. She became more like a sister to me than a cousin. She was always there for me. Whenever I had a problem, she was always there to listen and offer her wise advice. In today's world it is hard to find a really good listener and Jill was that. She was always willing to help in whatever way she could. Always cheerful and sweet, no matter what was going on in HER life.

Jill was a hard-working woman. She worked at **A & S for many years until she was in her 80's in** the Credit & Collections Department. This gives you an idea about her patience and rapport with people. She planted vegetables and flowers in her garden up until her 80's. She was a great cook and prepared dinners that were fit for a banquet. Jill was a very strong woman. She was not a complainer and whatever life dealt her, she carried on; even through the 2-1/2 years of being paralyzed and confined to her room due to cancer. Someone else might have easily gone stir-crazy. Throughout the years of pain and much discomfort she did not complain until the very end. She was a good mother and always concerned about her family's welfare. Although I miss Jill very much, her life on earth left much to emulate. When I think of her, I try to be a better listener and a more patient person.

SENDING A MESSAGE

We were treated to a beautiful sunrise as the bus left the parking lot from Temple Beth Sholom in Roslyn, Long Island. We were en route to Washington, D.C. on a December day to join the demonstration for Soviet Jewry to give clout to the Summit Meeting with Gorbachev the following day. This turned out to be the largest Jewish demonstration in American history. 250,000 people attended. I witnessed what appeared to be a never-ending, heavy stream of people marching down the steps of the Capital to an already crowded Mall filled with people farther than the eye could see. It was a beautiful sight to behold. It was like a scene from "Exodus" and the sign-bearers carrying slogans like "Let my people go!" gave it more credibility. People came from as far away as Hawaii, Colorado, Canada, etc. Both the young and the old were present. Considering the amount of people, it was remarkable that there were no reports of violence and I noticed that there was no pushing or shoving.

On the same day of the demonstration, there was also one being held in Russia by refuseniks and they were arrested and beaten. So much for "glasnost". I thank God that I live in a country where I am able to voice my opinions.

Attending the rally was a "high" in my life. I heard others voice the same feeling of "euphoria". My daughter Susan said being present made her realize how important each individual can be to form a unity in order to have strength to accomplish our important goals. My close friend, and Temple member, Judith Endlich, upon viewing the vast amount of people remarked that if this many Jews had been demonstrating in 1940, perhaps we would not have lost the Six Million. History has taught us that silence is not the road to take. Together with our actions and prayers, with the help of God, we were privileged to really witness an "Exodus" of Jews from Russia and religious freedom for those that wish to remain.

On another warm spring day, years later, I was again at a major demonstration at the capital in Washington. This time it was to show support for Israel suffering from a wave of suicide bombings occurring almost daily. Here again, it was considered to be the largest demonstration for Israel ever. People came from as far away as Alaska. Keith, my son-in law informed me of the demonstration just a few days before and Keith, and Judy and myself reserved seats on the bus. As we neared Washington, it was awesome to see buses converging from every direction and from every corner of the country. By our presence, we were sending a message to the world. I remember a Rabbi once mentioning that it is not enough for us to pray; that we must do all we can and God would meet us the rest of the way. After this demonstration, the Senate and the House voted tremendously in support of Israel. Hopefully, this time as with the Russian Jews, God and the world will hear our voice and our prayers will be answered so that Israel may enjoy true peace!

THE BUTTERFLY

Max and I were visiting our son Larry and daughter-in law Tsippy in Los Angeles. One Sabbath, we decided to attend their synagogue. The weather was warm and the synagogue doors were open. A beautiful Monarch butterfly flew into the sanctuary and alighted on the yarmulka of one of the congregants a few seats in front of me. Its beautiful colors blended into those of the yarmulka. The butterfly remained on the man's head almost throughout the services. He was unaware of this as other congregants took note of it and began whispering to each other about it. Toward the end of the service, the man stood up to say Kaddish which is the prayer recited in memory of a loved one who has passed away. The butterfly still remained on his head. After the

Kaddish was said, the butterfly flew away, out the door, not perching on anyone else.

When I witnessed this, my thoughts were that the butterfly must be the soul of the deceased person he was praying for.

A few years later, I saw a program on television about butterflies that paralleled the above-mentioned experience. A well-liked, handicapped child had passed away and his classmates were grieving for him. The teacher created a butterfly project to help the handicapped students get their minds off him. They were given plants and watched the caterpillars eat the plants and turn into Monarch butterflies. They decided to build a butterfly memorial garden for their friend. It took much work to do this, involving art, building, planting, etc. This helped the students to develop useful skills. At the time of dedication, a large number of Monarch butterflies were let loose and they all flew away. Except for one! It landed on the hair of the mother of the deceased boy. During the whole ceremony, it stayed on her head. When it was called to her attention, she began to cry. She felt it was the soul of her son visiting her and all his friends at this special time. There is a myth that Aztecs believed that the souls of the departed ride on the backs of the Monarch butterfly!

MESSAGES FROM SCRABBLE
A KITTEN

My youngest daughter Michelle had been the owner of two cats. One of them was an indoor cat that was timid and afraid to venture outdoors. The other one prowled the neighborhood fearlessly. One day she failed to return home. Weeks went by and there was no sign of her. After a few months, Michelle decided to get another kitten for the indoor cat was lonely. She had previously acquired the two cats from an animal shelter and decided that she would go there again. About one week before that visit, I was playing our usual Friday night scrabble game with Max, my cousin Hank and

Alice, my tenant. When I looked down at my tiles, "KITVET" was arranged on the rack. "KITVET"? I wondered. I knew Michelle was going to get a kitten, but I knew she intended to go to the animal shelter – not the vet. A week later she called after her visit to the shelter. She was very upset. She was unable to obtain a kitten from the shelter. I asked my friends if they knew anyone that wanted to give away a kitten but it was not the case. It seems that Murphy's Law stepped in. When one is not able to take in a cat, they are all over the place and seemed scarce when they are wanted. I remembered the message from my scrabble game wondering if veterinarians have cats for adoption. I called my vet and was surprised to hear that they had three kittens waiting to be taken! Michelle went over immediately to the vet, which was close to her home. I visited Michelle later that day. She was lying down and there was a small black ball of fluff perched on her chest looking very content and Michelle was all smiles. Glad I listened to my scrabble message!

SCRABBLE MESSAGE FOR MY BOOK

At one of these Friday night scrabble games, I was amazed to find the tiles on my rack arranged as follows: "MESAGES". I was unnerved because I had been lax about working on my book. I am sure this was a gentle reminder to get with it!

A WINNING MESSAGE

During one of these games, I had three tiles on my rack before I picked up the remaining four. I was stunned to find that they happened to be arranged to spell "GOD". When I added other four tiles, the seven tiles formed "GODWINU. I understood that to mean that I would win the game. However, throughout most of the game, I had the lowest score, and I could not see how I could possibly win. Toward the end though, I was surprised to find that I did win after all. I know this was merely a scrabble game; not of much significance. But I feel that God is telling me that when things are looking on the down side, not to give up hope!

"AS YOU SOW, SO SHALL YOU REAP"

As we were playing scrabble one evening, Max decided to change two of his tiles for hopefully better letters. He put the letters aside and went into the bag, and to his disappointment, retrieved the same type of letters as before. Immediately after, it was my turn and I placed two letters on the board to make a word. When I went to replace the two letters, they, too, were exactly the same type of letters as I had put on the board. This was too coincidental, I thought. It had to be a message! As I pondered it, I realized what it signified to me. What you put in that's what you get back! "As you sow, so shall you reap". I have noticed when I take my widowed or sick friends out shopping, I always wind up finding something special that I had been searching for. I would not have found these items had I not been taking them where they wanted to go.

SCRABBLE MESSAGES FROM ISRAEL (TRIP NO. 8)

My daughter Michelle accompanied me on this trip, since her husband, Sean, was too busy at work and Max felt he had obligations at home, which prevented the guys from coming with us. We took along a small travel scrabble game and whenever we would play, we would constantly receive messages that gave us a spooky feeling; almost like using an Ouija board, even though we were not seeking messages. They would just come to us.

There was the time we were sitting on the terrace of our hotel room in Eilat which overlooked beautiful palm trees and flora. Eilat is a resort built in the Negev desert. As we were playing scrabble, I was in awe of how such beauty could exist in the middle of the desert. When I looked down at the tiles on my scrabble rack, the word "oasis" was formed. Couldn't be more appropriate!

Michelle did not receive a call from Sean for several days and I could see that she was feeling a bit depressed. I tried to reassure her with "Sean is quite busy setting up his business and phone calls to Israel can be expensive". I could see that she still was not happy. While we were playing scrabble, she looked at her rack and "sean" was spelled out. "See" I consoled her. "He's thinking about you!"

As we continued the game, "seansea" tiles lined up on her rack. She put down the last "a" and picked up an "n" which would have spelled "Sean" twice! The next game we played, "sean" was again on the rack! It was later discovered that Sean had been trying to reach her by phone for several days and left messages. Michelle discovered later that the message light on the phone was not working. I believe his strong love for her managed to reach her through another channel.

As our trip was coming to a close, we were playing one last game of scrabble. We are both very much in love with Israel and having enjoyed our trip so much, we regretted leaving even though we missed our husbands. As I looked down on my scrabble rack, I noticed the letter formation, "srael" and I realized that the "I" was missing. As I would sadly be leaving Israel, I took the missing "I" to represent myself being removed from Israel!

WHAT'S IN A NAME?

During a Shabbat service several years ago, I was reading the Torah portion and my eyes for some reason moved to the opposite side of the page from which I was reading. Spots appeared on the bottom of that page and hovered over the name of Asher's grandson Malchiel. Not only was my attention called to our name in the Bible that morning but also my whole family received aliyahs that morning.

A few years later, several days before Max's 62nd birthday, he received an aliyah on Shabbat that contained the reading from the Torah of the name of Asher's grandson Malchiel. It seemed very strange that out of all the Aliyahs the one he was chosen for contained his name.

This had an extra special significance. During Michelle's Bat Mitzvah celebration in Israel, her Torah reading for that morning was the same Torah reading, which contained the name of Malchiel. The Rabbi in Israel, an old friend of ours, spoke of the Malkiel family in his sermon and made mention of the parallel. The choosing of the Torah reading for her Bat-Mitzvah was not planned. It just worked out that way. Coincidence? I doubt it!

By the way, the name Malkiel translated from the Hebrew means "God is my King!"

A TIMELY REMINDER

I was shopping for Chanuka gifts and a birthday gift for my grandson, Benjamin. I forgot my shopping list at home and could not recall one last item that I was planning to get for Benjamin. In my futile attempt to remember, I cruised the aisles of the department store searching in frustration. I was just about to give up and head for the door, when a young child passed me. He was seated in a shopping cart pushed by his mother and shouted "Mommy, I want a Thomas Train!" That was it! That was what Benjamin wanted for his birthday! I do believe that God and his angels help us in even what may seem to us the most trivial of things!

GOD WILL PROVIDE

When my grandson, Benjamin, was five years old, there was a conflict between Keith and Felicia of where their son should attend school. As Keith was becoming more religious, the Rabbi that he studied with approached him with how important it would be for Benjamin to receive a Jewish education. They applied to a Jewish Day School. Tuition was too high and the location was quite a distance away. Felicia did not want to risk the possibility of getting into debt in the future and Keith was upset for he wanted so much for Benjamin to have a religious education. One evening upon his return home from an evening prayer service, he quoted to Felicia a part of the "Shema" prayer which is found in the Bible that he had just been reading. "It says in the prayer to teach the commandments THOROUGHLY to your children and that if you follow the commandments and love God and serve Him with all your heart that He will provide 'rain for your land in its proper time, that you may gather in your grain, your wine and your oil and you will eat and be satisfied.' So you see, Felicia, we have to have faith that God will provide and send Benjamin to Hebrew School so that he can be taught thoroughly like it says in the "Shema"! But, even with all of the school's offers, Felicia still did not want to send Benjamin for fear of getting into debt. Benjamin was finally enrolled in the local public school much to Keith's and my own disappointment.

Summer passed and it was one week prior to when Benjamin was to start Kindergarten that Felicia received information that a new Hebrew Day School was opening. It was just about a mile away from her home. At the same time, Keith received a long-awaited raise that was the same amount as the tuition. The school was now affordable! Our family was ecstatic! Benjamin would be able to get his "thorough" education! He would also be able to progress according to his ability for the classes would be divided in groups according to the children's capabilities. This was important for at the age of five, Benjamin could already read quite fluently.

Well, God was providing the "grain, the wine and the oil" when it was least expected! A little faith goes a long way! Baruch Hashem!

Chapter 18:

THE ZOHAR

For some time, I have been interested in Kabala (Jewish Mysticism). Kabala is derived from the Zohar which is a mystical text based on the Torah. It contains the teachings of a well-known Rabbi, Simon bar Yochai, who lived in the second century. The Zohar is written in Aramaic and consists of many volumes, broken down into the sections (parshas) of the Torah that are read consecutively each week in the synagogue. It is thought that even if one does not understand the Aramaic, just scanning the text for the particular week, can bring that person, at that time, a special energy and even make ones prayers more powerful.

I own the Zohar and during the week I read the Bible portion that will be read in the synagogue during the coming Sabbath. After that, I scan the Zohar that contains the portion for that week. Since I have the Zohar, I have experienced some strange episodes pertaining to it.

I was informed when I purchased the Zohar that some of the books have particular energies for specific areas of our lives. For instance, the section on Pinchas is said to bring healing. When I am using this book when I pray for the sick, I seem to have a better response. Book Four is designated for safety in travel. We were advised to place this volume in the back of our car. One day, Max and I were driving our grandson to our home. We were on the Long Island Expressway and suddenly Max felt the breaks of the car give way as he was driving. We were approximately seven miles from our exit. Max nervously slowed down the speed of the car as much as he could and we prayed fervently. He managed to get us off to the exit and drove into the parking lot of the Syosset library and was somehow able to get the car to crawl to a stop. Baruch Hashem! My young grandson, unaware of how dangerous a situation this could have been, was all in awe watching the tow truck haul our car away. Max is not much into Kabala, but after this episode, he will not travel without the special "Book Four" in the back of his car!

During another incident, my youngest daughter Michelle and I had an argument and she packed up her belongings and left, storming out of the house without letting us know where she was going. She was about 19 years old at the time. I spent a very troubled evening worrying about her whereabouts. I prayed that she would be all right and picked up the Zohar and scanned a paragraph hoping that the scanning would open the channels for my prayers. Just then the phone rang! It was Michelle, letting me know she was all right; that she was at a friend's house. "I love you Mom and I am sorry that I upset you" was her message. I sobbed with relief! I went to sleep that evening feeling at peace and thanked God.

Chapter 19:

On 9/11

After this horrible episode, it seems that it has made some people stronger, more appreciative of life and more helpful to each other. In all tragedies, some good usually comes of it. After the Holocaust, the State of Israel was born. During and after 9/11, great heroism was shown. Many people banded together to give blood and gave charity, devoted their time to help and risked their lives to save others.

However, it has also made some more skeptical about God. Where was God? The same question arose during the Holocaust. We must remember that God has granted us free will. We cannot blame God for the evil actions of some people. We also cannot blame God for those who stand idly by when they could do something to avoid tragedy to other people. I had a conversation with someone who questioned why God gave us free will altogether. "Why didn't God make us all good so that we could live in peace?" she asked. If everything that we had was just given to us without any effort on our part to earn it, I imagine life would be meaningless. The next question is, why are good people, some so young, taken from life, without any seemingly good explanation? In Judaism, we are taught that God gave the Torah to us and "It is not in heaven, but on earth for us to explore its teachings and Commandments". However, the things, we cannot fathom, we are told, are known only to God. Since God is the all-knowing creator of our body and our souls, only He knows when our souls will depart and what happens in the hereafter. According to Kabalah, we are believed to be here to make correction for our past lives (tikune). I remember reading that the human brain is much too large and a good part of it appears empty. Perhaps the "empty" parts contain information of the souls from past lives. In each life, we are supposed to be planted in a select surrounding that would enable us to make up our corrections easier. I believe when the soul completes its tikune, it goes to "heaven". If not, it is placed in another life again in a different surrounding to try again, sometimes for many rebirths. I believe the "angels" are souls that have completed their tikune and are sent to earth to help other souls reach their corrections and to protect them.

On our return from Israel during the summer of 2001, I was discussing our trip with a Temple member during a gathering. She had also visited Israel that summer and had enjoyed it immensely. A few other members joined the conversation and voiced the opinion that we had taken a great risk by going. I retorted with what was almost prophecy. "What makes you think you are so safe in this country? I don 't feel very safe when I go to Manhattan. And what about the bombing of the World Trade Center a few years ago, the Oklahoma bombing and schools being terrorized?" (This conversation took place one week before the Sept. 11 disaster) The response to this was "Oh, that happened a while ago and if someone told you to jump off the roof you don't have to do it!"

"I don't think going to Israel should be compared to jumping off the roof" I answered "and if I have a chance to help and enjoy Israel, I am not going to let terrorism stop me!" My answer to the congregants, was sad to say, repeated by President Bush and Mayor Guiliani a few weeks later after the World Trade Center disaster of Sept. 11 when they advised the country to "go on with your life" and don't allow terrorism to take us over with fear. Israel, now and for many years has had to live with terrorism every day of their lives, not knowing when and where a suicide bomber will strike. But they go on with their lives!

A few days before September 11, my daughter Felicia decided to take a picture of the Manhattan skyline as she traveled on the Brooklyn-Queens Expressway. Of course this view included the World Trade Center. She had passed this view many times before. Was it a psychic decision?

It seems that the 9/11 attack has drawn the people of the US closer together to become a stronger nation

344

against terror that threatens the whole world. Together, with God's help, we will succeed!

Chapter 20:

IN CONCLUSION

It is my hope that the reader will find a parallel in these episodes in their own lives and be spurred on to analyze and act upon their *own* messages.

A message comes to me from the Prophet Isaiah, Chapter 43, Verse 10: "Ye are my witnesses" saith the Lord.' If God has chosen to "open my eyes" with these experiences, that obligates me to share it with others in order for us to ALL be "His witnesses" every day of our lives.

About The Author

A native of New York, the author is a mother of five children, six grandchildren and has been happily married 45 years. As a child, the author had a gift for writing. However, that talent was put on hold so that she could take care of her parents and then raise her family.

The author draws on her life experiences to demonstrate how God became her therapist, physician and guide through messages received.

Printed in the United States
52660LVS00001B/7-24

9 781420 837407